Environmental Issues

CONSERVATION

Environmental Issues

AIR QUALITY
CLIMATE CHANGE
CONSERVATION
ENVIRONMENTAL POLICY
WATER POLLUTION
WILDLIFE PROTECTION

Environmental Issues

CONSERVATION

Yael Calhoun
Series Editor

Foreword by David Seideman,
Editor-in-Chief, *Audubon* Magazine

CHELSEA HOUSE
PUBLISHERS
A Haights Cross Communications Company ®
Philadelphia

CHELSEA HOUSE PUBLISHERS
VP, New Product Development Sally Cheney
Director of Production Kim Shinners
Creative Manager Takeshi Takahashi
Manufacturing Manager Diann Grasse

Staff for CONSERVATION
Executive Editor Tara Koellhoffer
Editorial Assistant Kuorkor Dzani
Production Editor Noelle Nardone
Photo Editor Sarah Bloom
Series and Cover Designer Keith Trego
Layout 21st Century Publishing and Communications, Inc.

A Haights Cross Communications ⚑ Company ®

First Printing

9 8 7 6 5 4 3 2 1

Library of Congress Cataloging-in-Publication Data.

Conservation / [edited by Yael Calhoun] ; foreword by David Seideman.
       p. cm. -- (Environmental issues)
   Includes bibliographical references and index.
   ISBN 0-7910-8203-2
1.   Conservation of natural resources--Juvenile literature. 2. Nature
conservation--Juvenile literature. I. Calhoun, Yael . II . Series.
   S940 . C63 2005
   333 . 72--dc22
                                                         2005003661

Contents Overview

Foreword by David Seideman, Editor-in-Chief, *Audubon* Magazine   viii

Introduction: "Why Should We Care?"   xiv

Section A:
Conservation Issues and Challenges   1

Section B:
The Oceans   47

Section C:
Rivers, Lakes, and Streams   87

Section D:
Federal Lands   115

Section E:
People in Conservation   137

Bibliography   153

Further Reading   154

Index   155

Detailed Table of Contents

Foreword by David Seideman, Editor-in-Chief, *Audubon* Magazine viii

Introduction: "Why Should We Care?" xiv

Section A:
Conservation Issues and Challenges 1

Does It Matter if Plants and Animals Go Extinct? 2

The Future of Life 3
by E. O. Wilson

How Did the Environmental Movement
Get Started in Our Country? 22

"The Story Until Now" 23
by Philip Shabecoff

How Does Growing Organic Coffee and
Chocolate Help Birds? 37

Made in the Shade 38
by Paul Tolme

Section B:
The Oceans 47

Do We Need to Protect Our Oceans? 48

**America's Living Oceans: Charting a
Course for Sea Change** 49
from the Pew Oceans Commission

Why Are Coral Reefs So Important to People
and to the Environment? 55

Rescuing Reefs in Hot Water 56
by Soames Summerhays

Can People Take Too Much From the Oceans? 65

The Empty Ocean 66
by Richard Ellis

Section C:
Rivers, Lakes, and Streams 87

Why Are Healthy Rivers Important to People? 88

Rivers for Life 89
by Sandra Postel and Brian Richter

Is There Enough Freshwater for Both Human
   Use and the Habitats That Support Plants
   and Animals? 103
   A Human Thirst 104
   by Don Hinrichsen

Section D:
Federal Lands 115

Why Does the Federal Government Want to Save
   the Everglades, the Largest Freshwater Marsh
   in the United States? 116
   "Reviving a River of Grass" 117
   by Ted Levin

Can We Protect the Wildlife and Habitat Around
   Yellowstone National Park? 125
   The Lone Rangers 126
   by William Stolzenburg

Section E:
People in Conservation 137

How Did the Writings of Rachel Carson Make
   Conservation a Household Word? 138
   Silent Spring 139
   by Rachel Carson

Why Are Volunteers out Looking for Frogs and
   Salamanders Every Spring? 145
   The Frog Squad 146
   by Christine Parrish

Bibliography 153
Further Reading 154
Index 155

FOREWORD

by David Seideman, Editor-in-Chief, *Audubon* Magazine

For anyone contemplating the Earth's fate, there's probably no more instructive case study than the Florida Everglades. When European explorers first arrived there in the mid-1800s, they discovered a lush, tropical wilderness with dense sawgrass, marshes, mangrove forests, lakes, and tree islands. By the early 20th century, developers and politicians had begun building a series of canals and dikes to siphon off the region's water. They succeeded in creating an agricultural and real estate boom, and to some degree, they offset floods and droughts. But the ecological cost was exorbitant. Today, half of the Everglades' wetlands have been lost, its water is polluted by runoff from farms, and much of its wildlife, including Florida panthers and many wading birds such as wood storks, are hanging on by a thread.

Yet there has been a renewed sense of hope in the Everglades since 2001, when the state of Florida and the federal government approved a comprehensive $7.8 billion restoration plan, the biggest recovery of its kind in history. During the next four decades, ecologists and engineers will work to undo years of ecological damage by redirecting water back into the Everglades' dried-up marshes. "The Everglades are a test," says Joe Podger, an environmentalist. "If we pass, we get to keep the planet."

In fact, as this comprehensive series on environmental issues shows, humankind faces a host of tests that will determine whether we get to keep the planet. The world's crises—air and water pollution, the extinction of species, and climate change—are worsening by the day. The solutions—and there are many practical ones—all demand an extreme sense of urgency. E. O. Wilson, the noted Harvard zoologist, contends that "the world environment is changing so fast that there is a window of opportunity that will close in as little time as the next two or three decades." While Wilson's main concern is the rapid loss of biodiversity, he could have just as easily been discussing climate change or wetlands destruction.

The Earth is suffering the most massive extinction of species since the die-off of dinosaurs 65 million years ago. "If we continue at the current rate of deforestation and destruction of major ecosystems like rain forests and coral reefs, where most of the biodiversity is concentrated," Wilson says, "we will surely lose more than half of all the species of plants and animals on Earth by the end of the 21st century."

Many conservationists still mourn the loss of the passenger pigeon, which, as recently as the late 1800s, flew in miles-long flocks so dense they blocked the sun, turning noontime into nighttime. By 1914, target shooters and market hunters had reduced the species to a single individual, Martha, who lived at the Cincinnati Zoo until, as Peter Matthiessen wrote in *Wildlife in America,* "she blinked for the last time." Despite U.S. laws in place to avert other species from going the way of the passenger pigeon, the latest news is still alarming. In its 2004 State of the Birds report, Audubon noted that 70% of grassland bird species and 36% of shrubland bird species are suffering significant declines. Like the proverbial canary in the coalmine, birds serve as indicators, sounding the alarm about impending threats to environmental and human health.

Besides being an unmitigated moral tragedy, the disappearance of species has profound practical implications. Ninety percent of the world's food production now comes from about a dozen species of plants and eight species of livestock. Geneticists rely on wild populations to replenish varieties of domestic corn, wheat, and other crops, and to boost yields and resistance to disease. "Nature is a natural pharmacopoeia, and new drugs and medicines are being discovered in the wild all the time," wrote Niles Eldredge of the American Museum of Natural History, a noted author on the subject of extinction. "Aspirin comes from the bark of willow trees. Penicillin comes from a mold, a type of fungus." Furthermore, having a wide array of plants and animals improves a region's capacity to cleanse water, enrich soil, maintain stable climates, and produce the oxygen we breathe.

Today, the quality of the air we breathe and the water we drink does not augur well for our future health and well-being. Many people assume that the passage of the Clean Air Act in 1970 ushered in a new age. But the American Lung Association reports that 159 million Americans—55% of the population—are exposed to "unhealthy levels of air pollution." Meanwhile, the American Heart Association warns of a direct link between exposure to air pollution and heart disease and strokes. While it's true that U.S. waters are cleaner than they were three decades ago, data from the Environmental Protection Agency (EPA) shows that almost half of U.S. coastal waters fail to meet water-quality standards because they cannot support fishing or swimming. Each year, contaminated tap water makes as many as 7 million Americans sick. The chief cause is "non-point pollution," runoff that includes fertilizers and pesticides from farms and backyards as well as oil and chemical spills. On a global level, more than a billion people lack access to clean water; according to the United Nations, five times that number die each year from malaria and other illnesses associated with unsafe water.

Of all the Earth's critical environmental problems, one trumps the rest: climate change. Carol Browner, the EPA's chief from 1993 through 2001 (the longest term in the agency's history), calls climate change "the greatest environmental health problem the world has ever seen." Industry and people are spewing carbon dioxide from smokestacks and the tailpipes of their cars into the atmosphere, where a buildup of gases, acting like the glass in a greenhouse, traps the sun's heat. The 1990s was the warmest decade in more than a century, and 1998 saw the highest global temperatures ever. In an article about global climate change in the December 2003 issue of *Audubon*, David Malakoff wrote, "Among the possible consequences: rising sea levels that cause coastal communities to sink beneath the waves like a modern Atlantis, crop failures of biblical proportions, and once-rare killer storms that start to appear with alarming regularity."

Yet for all the doom and gloom, scientists and environmentalists hold out hope. When Russia recently ratified the Kyoto Protocol, it meant that virtually all of the world's industrialized nations—the United States, which has refused to sign, is a notable exception—have committed to cutting greenhouse gases. As Kyoto and other international agreements go into effect, a market is developing for cap-and-trade systems for carbon dioxide. In this country, two dozen big corporations, including British Petroleum, are cutting emissions. At least 28 American states have adopted their own policies. California, for example, has passed global warming legislation aimed at curbing emissions from new cars. Governor Arnold Schwarzenegger has also backed regulations requiring automakers to slash the amount of greenhouse gases they cause by up to 30% by 2016, setting a precedent for other states.

As Washington pushes a business-friendly agenda, states are filling in the policy vacuum in other areas, as well. California and New York are developing laws to preserve wetlands, which filter pollutants, prevent floods, and provide habitat for endangered wildlife.

By taking matters into their own hands, states and foreign countries will ultimately force Washington's. What industry especially abhors is a crazy quilt of varying rules. After all, it makes little sense for a company to invest a billion dollars in a power plant only to find out later that it has to spend even more to comply with another state's stricter emissions standards. Ford chairman and chief executive William Ford has lashed out at the states' "patchwork" approach because he and "other manufacturers will have a hard time responding." Further, he wrote in a letter to his company's top managers, "the prospect of 50 different requirements in 50 different states would be nothing short of chaos." The type of fears Ford expresses are precisely the reason federal laws protecting clean air and water came into being.

Governments must take the lead, but ecologically conscious consumers wield enormous influence, too. Over the past four decades, the annual use of pesticides has more than doubled, from 215 million pounds to 511 million pounds. Each year, these poisons cause $10 billion worth of damage to the environment and kill 72 million birds. The good news is that the demand for organic products is revolutionizing agriculture, in part by creating a market for natural alternatives for pest control. Some industry experts predict that by 2007 the organic industry will almost quadruple, to more than $30 billion.

E. O. Wilson touts "shade-grown" coffee as one of many "personal habitats that, if moderated only in this country, could contribute significantly to saving endangered species." In the mountains of Mexico and Central America, coffee grown beneath a dense forest canopy rather than in cleared fields helps provide refuge for dozens of wintering North American migratory bird species, from western tanagers to Baltimore orioles.

With conservation such a huge part of Americans' daily routine, recycling has become as ingrained a civic duty as obeying traffic lights. Californians, for their part, have cut their energy consumption by 10% each year since the state's 2001 energy crisis. "Poll after poll shows that about two-thirds of the American public—Democrat and Republican, urban and rural—consider environmental progress crucial," writes Carl Pope, director of the Sierra Club, in his recent book, *Strategic Ignorance*. "Clean air, clean water, wilderness preservation—these are such bedrock values that many polling respondents find it hard to believe that any politician would oppose them."

Terrorism and the economy clearly dwarfed all other issues in the 2004 presidential election. Even so, voters approved 120 out of 161 state and local conservation funding measures nationwide, worth a total of $3.25 billion. Anti-environment votes in the U.S. Congress and proposals floated by the like-minded Bush administration should not obscure the salient fact that so far there have been no changes to the major environmental laws. The potential for political fallout is too great.

The United States' legacy of preserving its natural heritage is the envy of the world. Our national park system alone draws more than 300 million visitors each year. Less well known is the 103-year-old national wildlife refuge system you'll learn about in this series. Its unique mission is to safeguard the nation's wild animals and plants on 540 refuges, protecting 700 species of birds and an equal number of other vertebrates; 282 of these species are either threatened or endangered. One of the many species particularly dependent on the invaluable habitat refuges afford is the bald eagle. Such safe havens, combined with the banning of the insecticide DDT and enforcement of the

Endangered Species Act, have led to the bald eagle's remarkable recovery, from a low of 500 breeding pairs in 1963 to 7,600 today. In fact, this bird, the national symbol of the United States, is about be removed from the endangered species list and downgraded to a less threatened status under the CITES, the Convention on International Trade in Endangered Species.

This vital treaty, upheld by the United States and 165 other participating nations (and detailed in this series), underscores the worldwide will to safeguard much of the Earth's magnificent wildlife. Since going into effect in 1975, CITES has helped enact plans to save tigers, chimpanzees, and African elephants. These species and many others continue to face dire threats from everything from poaching to deforestation. At the same time, political progress is still being made. Organizations like the World Wildlife Fund work tirelessly to save these species from extinction because so many millions of people care. China, for example, the most populous nation on Earth, is so concerned about its giant pandas that it has implemented an ambitious captive breeding program. That program's success, along with government measures prohibiting logging throughout the panda's range, may actually enable the remaining population of 1,600 pandas to hold its own—and perhaps grow. "For the People's Republic of China, pressure intensified as its internationally popular icon edged closer to extinction," wrote Gerry Ellis in a recent issue of *National Wildlife*. "The giant panda was not only a poster child for endangered species, it was a symbol of our willingness to ensure nature's place on Earth."

Whether people take a spiritual path to conservation or a pragmatic one, they ultimately arrive at the same destination. The sight of a bald eagle soaring across the horizon reassures us about nature's resilience, even as the clean air and water we both need to survive becomes less of a certainty. "The conservation of our natural resources and their proper use constitute the fundamental problem which underlies almost every other problem of our national life," President Theodore Roosevelt told Congress at the dawn of the conservation movement a century ago. His words ring truer today than ever.

Introduction: "Why Should We Care?"

Our nation's air and water are cleaner today than they were 30 years ago. After a century of filling and destroying over half of our wetlands, we now protect many of them. But the Earth is getting warmer, habitats are being lost to development and logging, and humans are using more water than ever before. Increased use of water can leave rivers, lakes, and wetlands without enough water to support the native plant and animal life. Such changes are causing plants and animals to go extinct at an increased rate. It is no longer a question of losing just the dodo birds or the passenger pigeons, argues David Quammen, author of *Song of the Dodo*: "Within a few decades, if present trends continue, we'll be losing *a lot* of everything." [1]

In the 1980s, E. O. Wilson, a Harvard biologist and Pulitzer Prize–winning author, helped bring the term *biodiversity* into public discussions about conservation. *Biodiversity*, short for "biological diversity," refers to the levels of organization for living things. Living organisms are divided and categorized into ecosystems (such as rain forests or oceans), by species (such as mountain gorillas), and by genetics (the genes responsible for inherited traits).

Wilson has predicted that if we continue to destroy habitats and pollute the Earth at the current rate, in 50 years, we could lose 30 to 50% of the planet's species to extinction. In his 1992 book, *The Diversity of Life*, Wilson asks: "Why should we care?" [2] His long list of answers to this question includes: the potential loss of vast amounts of scientific information that would enable the development of new crops, products, and medicines and the potential loss of the vast economic and environmental benefits of healthy ecosystems. He argues that since we have only a vague idea (even with our advanced scientific methods) of how ecosystems really work, it would be "reckless" to suppose that destroying species indefinitely will not threaten us all in ways we may not even understand.

THE BOOKS IN THE SERIES

In looking at environmental issues, it quickly becomes clear that, as naturalist John Muir once said, "When we try to pick out anything by itself, we find it hitched to everything else in the Universe."[3] For example, air pollution in one state or in one country can affect not only air quality in another place, but also land and water quality. Soil particles from degraded African lands can blow across the ocean and cause damage to far-off coral reefs.

The six books in this series address a variety of environmental issues: conservation, wildlife protection, water pollution, air quality, climate change, and environmental policy. None of these can be viewed as a separate issue. Air quality impacts climate change, wildlife, and water quality. Conservation initiatives directly affect water and air quality, climate change, and wildlife protection. Endangered species are touched by each of these issues. And finally, environmental policy issues serve as important tools in addressing all the other environmental problems that face us.

You can use the burning of coal as an example to look at how a single activity directly "hitches" to a variety of environmental issues. Humans have been burning coal as a fuel for hundreds of years. The mining of coal can leave the land stripped of vegetation, which erodes the soil. Soil erosion contributes to particulates in the air and water quality problems. Mining coal can also leave piles of acidic tailings that degrade habitats and pollute water. Burning any fossil fuel—coal, gas, or oil—releases large amounts of carbon dioxide into the atmosphere. Carbon dioxide is considered a major "greenhouse gas" that contributes to global warming—the gradual increase in the Earth's temperature over time. In addition, coal burning adds sulfur dioxide to the air, which contributes to the formation of acid rain—precipitation that is abnormally acidic. This acid rain can kill forests and leave lakes too acidic to support life. Technology continues to present ways to minimize the pollution that results from extracting and burning fossil fuels. Clean air and climate change policies guide states and industries toward implementing various strategies and technologies for a cleaner coal industry.

Each of the six books in this series—ENVIRONMENTAL ISSUES—introduces the significant points that relate to the specific topic and explains its relationship to other environmental concerns.

Book One: *Air Quality*

Problems of air pollution can be traced back to the time when humans first started to burn coal. *Air Quality* looks at today's challenges in fighting to keep our air clean and safe. The book includes discussions of air pollution sources—car and truck emissions, diesel engines, and many industries. It also discusses their effects on our health and the environment.

The Environmental Protection Agency (EPA) has reported that more than 150 million Americans live in areas that have unhealthy levels of some type of air pollution.[4] Today, more than 20 million Americans, over 6 million of whom are children, suffer from asthma believed to be triggered by pollutants in the air.[5]

In 1970, Congress passed the Clean Air Act, putting in place an ambitious set of regulations to address air pollution concerns. The EPA has identified and set standards for six common air pollutants: ground-level ozone, nitrogen oxides, particulate matter, sulfur dioxide, carbon monoxide, and lead.

The EPA has also been developing the Clean Air Rules of 2004, national standards aimed at improving the country's air quality by specifically addressing the many sources of contaminants. However, many conservation organizations and even some states have concerns over what appears to be an attempt to weaken different sections of the 1990 version of the Clean Air Act. The government's environmental protection efforts take on increasing importance because air pollution degrades land and water, contributes to global warming, and affects the health of plants and animals, including humans.

Book Two: *Climate Change*

Part of science is observing patterns, and scientists have observed a global rise in temperature. *Climate Change* discusses the sources and effects of global warming. Scientists attribute this accelerated change to human activities such as the burning of fossil fuels that emit greenhouse gases (GHG).[6] Since the 1700s, we have been cutting down the trees that help remove carbon dioxide from the atmosphere, and have increased the amount of coal, gas, and oil we burn, all of which add carbon dioxide to the atmosphere. Science tells us that these human activities have caused greenhouse gases—carbon dioxide (CO_2), methane (CH_4), nitrous oxide (N_2O), hydrofluorocarbons (HFCs), perfluorocarbons (PFCs), and sulfur hexafluoride (SF_6)—to accumulate in the atmosphere.[7]

If the warming patterns continue, scientists warn of more negative environmental changes. The effects of climate change, or global warming, can be seen all over the world. Thousands of scientists are predicting rising sea levels, disturbances in patterns of rainfall and regional weather, and changes in ranges and reproductive cycles of plants and animals. Climate change is already having some effects on certain plant and animal species.[8]

Many countries and some American states are already working together and with industries to reduce the emissions of greenhouse gases. Climate change is an issue that clearly fits noted scientist Rene Dubois's advice: "Think globally, act locally."

Book Three: *Conservation*

Conservation considers the issues that affect our world's vast array of living creatures and the land, water, and air they need to survive.

One of the first people in the United States to put the political spotlight on conservation ideas was President Theodore Roosevelt. In the early 1900s, he formulated policies and created programs that addressed his belief that: "The nation behaves well if it treats the natural resources as assets which it must turn over to the next generation increased, and not impaired, in value."[9] In the 1960s, biologist Rachel Carson's book, *Silent Spring*, brought conservation issues into the public eye. People began to see that polluted land, water, and air affected their health. The 1970s brought the creation of the United States Environmental Protection Agency (EPA) and passage of many federal and state rules and regulations to protect the quality of our environment and our health.

Some 80 years after Theodore Roosevelt established the first National Wildlife Refuge in 1903, Harvard biologist

E. O. Wilson brought public awareness of conservation issues to a new level. He warned:

> . . . the worst thing that will probably happen—in fact is already well underway—is not energy depletion, economic collapse, conventional war, or even the expansion of totalitarian governments. As terrible as these catastrophes would be for us, they can be repaired within a few generations. The one process now ongoing that will take million of years to correct is the loss of genetic species diversity by the destruction of natural habitats. This is the folly our descendants are least likely to forgive us.[10]

To heed Wilson's warning means we must strive to protect species-rich habitats, or "hotspots," such as tropical rain forests and coral reefs. It means dealing with conservation concerns like soil erosion and pollution of fresh water and of the oceans. It means protecting sea and land habitats from the overexploitation of resources. And it means getting people involved on all levels—from national and international government agencies, to private conservation organizations, to the individual person who recycles or volunteers to listen for the sounds of frogs in the spring.

Book Four: *Environmental Policy*

One approach to solving environmental problems is to develop regulations and standards of safety. Just as there are rules for living in a community or for driving on a road, there are environmental regulations and policies that work toward protecting our health and our lands. *Environmental Policy* discusses the regulations and programs that have been crafted to address environmental issues at all levels—global, national, state, and local.

Today, as our resources become increasingly limited, we witness heated debates about how to use our public lands and how to protect the quality of our air and water. Should we allow drilling in the Arctic National Wildlife Refuge? Should we protect more marine areas? Should we more closely regulate the emissions of vehicles, ships, and industries? These policy issues, and many more, continue to make news on a daily basis.

In addition, environmental policy has taken a place on the international front. Hundreds of countries are working together in a variety of ways to address such issues as global warming, air pollution, water pollution and supply, land preservation, and the protection of endangered species. One question the United States continues to debate is whether to sign the 1997 Kyoto Protocol, the international agreement designed to decrease the emissions of greenhouse gases.

Many of the policy tools for protecting our environment are already in place. It remains a question how they will be used— and whether they will be put into action in time to save our natural resources and ourselves.

Book Five: *Water Pollution*

Pollution can affect water everywhere. Pollution in lakes and rivers is easily seen. But water that is out of our plain view can also be polluted with substances such as toxic chemicals, fertilizers, pesticides, oils, and gasoline. *Water Pollution* considers issues of concern to our surface waters, our groundwater, and our oceans.

In the early 1970s, about three-quarters of the water in the United States was considered unsafe for swimming and fishing. When Lake Erie was declared "dead" from pollution and a river feeding it actually caught on fire, people decided that the national government had to take a stronger role in protecting our resources. In 1972, Congress passed the Clean Water Act, a law whose objective "is to restore and maintain the chemical, physical, and biological integrity of the Nation's waters."[11] Today, over 30 years later, many lakes and rivers have been restored to health. Still, an estimated 40% of our waters are still unsafe to swim in or fish.

Less than 1% of the available water on the planet is fresh water. As the world's population grows, our demand for drinking and irrigation water increases. Therefore, the quantity of available water has become a major global issue. As Sandra Postel, a leading authority on international freshwater issues, says, "Water scarcity is now the single biggest threat to global food production."[12] Because there are many competing demands for water, including the needs of habitats, water pollution continues to become an even more serious problem each year.

Book Six: *Wildlife Protection*

For many years, the word *wildlife* meant only the animals that people hunted for food or for sport. It was not until 1986 that the Oxford English Dictionary defined *wildlife* as "the native fauna and flora of a particular region."[13] *Wildlife Protection* looks at overexploitation—for example, overfishing or collecting plants and animals for illegal trade—and habitat loss. Habitat loss can be the result of development, logging, pollution, water diverted for human use, air pollution, and climate change.

Also discussed are various approaches to wildlife protection. Since protection of wildlife is an issue of global concern, it is addressed here on international as well as on national and local levels. Topics include voluntary international organizations such as the International Whaling Commission and the CITES agreements on trade in endangered species. In the United States, the Endangered Species Act provides legal protection for more than 1,200 different plant and animal species. Another approach to wildlife protection includes developing partnerships among conservation organizations, governments, and local people to foster economic incentives to protect wildlife.

CONSERVATION IN THE UNITED STATES

Those who first lived on this land, the Native American peoples, believed in general that land was held in common, not to be individually owned, fenced, or tamed. The white settlers from Europe had very different views of land. Some believed the New World was a Garden of Eden. It was a land of opportunity for them, but it was also a land to be controlled and subdued. Ideas on how to treat the land often followed those of European thinkers like John Locke, who believed that "Land that is left wholly to nature is called, as indeed it is, waste." [14]

The 1800s brought another way of approaching the land. Thinkers such as Ralph Waldo Emerson, John Muir, and Henry David Thoreau celebrated our human connection with nature. By the end of the 1800s, some scientists and policymakers were noticing the damage humans have caused to the land. Leading public officials preached stewardship and wise use of our country's resources. In 1873, Yellowstone National Park was set up. In 1903, the first National Wildlife Refuge was established.

However, most of the government practices until the middle of the 20th century favored unregulated development and use of the land's resources. Forests were clear cut, rivers were dammed, wetlands were filled to create farmland, and factories were allowed to dump their untreated waste into rivers and lakes.

In 1949, a forester and ecologist named Aldo Leopold revived the concept of preserving land for its own sake. But there was now a biological, or scientific, reason for conservation, not just a spiritual one. Leopold declared: "All ethics rest upon a single premise: that the individual is a member of a community of interdependent parts. . . . A thing is right when it tends to preserve the integrity and stability and beauty of the biotic community. It is wrong when it tends otherwise." [15]

The fiery vision of these conservationists helped shape a more far-reaching movement that began in the 1960s. Many credit Rachel Carson's eloquent and accessible writings, such as her 1962 book *Silent Spring*, with bringing environmental issues into people's everyday language. When the Cuyahoga River in Ohio caught fire in 1969 because it was so polluted, it captured the public attention. Conservation was no longer just about protecting land that many people would never even see, it was about protecting human health. The condition of the environment had become personal.

In response to the public outcry about water and air pollution, the 1970s saw the establishment of the EPA. Important legislation to protect the air and water was passed. National standards for a cleaner environment were set and programs were established to help achieve the ambitious goals. Conservation organizations grew from what had started as exclusive white men's hunting clubs to interest groups with a broad membership base. People came together to demand changes that would afford more protection to the environment and to their health.

Since the 1960s, some presidential administrations have sought to strengthen environmental protection and to protect more land and national treasures. For example, in 1980, President Jimmy Carter signed an act that doubled the amount of protected land in Alaska and renamed it the Arctic National Wildlife Refuge. Other administrations, like those of President Ronald Reagan, sought to dismantle many earlier environmental protection initiatives.

The environmental movement, or environmentalism, is not one single, homogeneous cause. The agencies, individuals, and organizations that work toward protecting the environment vary as widely as the habitats and places they seek to protect. There are individuals who begin grass-roots efforts—people like Lois Marie Gibbs, a former resident of the polluted area of Love Canal, New York, who founded the Center for Health, Environment and Justice. There are conservation organizations, like The Nature Conservancy, the World Wildlife Fund (WWF), and Conservation International, that sponsor programs to preserve and protect habitats. There are groups that specialize in monitoring public policy and legislation—for example, the Natural Resources Defense Council and Environmental Defense. In addition, there are organizations like the Audubon Society and the National Wildlife Federation whose focus is on public education about environmental issues. Perhaps from this diversity, just like there exists in a healthy ecosystem, will come the strength and vision environmentalism needs to deal with the continuing issues of the 21st century.

INTERNATIONAL CONSERVATION EFFORTS

In his book *Biodiversity*, E. O. Wilson cautions that biological diversity must be taken seriously as a global resource for three reasons. First, human population growth is accelerating the degrading of the environment, especially in tropical countries. Second, science continues to discover new uses for biological diversity—uses that can benefit human health and protect the environment. And third, much biodiversity is being lost through extinction, much of it in the tropics. As Wilson states, "We must hurry to acquire the knowledge on which a wise policy of conservation and development can be based for centuries to come."[16]

People organize themselves within boundaries and borders. But oceans, rivers, air, and wildlife do not follow such rules. Pollution or overfishing in one part of an ocean can easily degrade the quality of another country's resources. If one country diverts a river, it can destroy another country's wetlands or water resources. When Wilson cautions us that we must hurry to develop a wise conservation policy, he means a policy that will protect resources all over the world.

To accomplish this will require countries to work together on critical global issues: preserving biodiversity, reducing global warming, decreasing air pollution, and protecting the oceans. There are many important international efforts already going on to protect the resources of our planet. Some efforts are regulatory, while others are being pursued by nongovernmental organizations or private conservation groups.

Countries volunteering to cooperate to protect resources is not a new idea. In 1946, a group of countries established the International Whaling Commission (IWC). They recognized that unregulated whaling around the world had led to severe declines in the world's whale populations. In 1986, the IWC declared a moratorium on whaling, which is still in effect, until the populations have recovered.[17] Another example of international cooperation occurred in 1987 when various countries signed the Montreal Protocol to reduce the emissions of ozone-depleting gases. It has been a huge success, and perhaps has served as a model for other international efforts, like the 1997 Kyoto Protocol, to limit emissions of greenhouse gases.

Yet another example of international environmental cooperation is the CITES agreement (the Convention on International Trade in Endangered Species of Wild Fauna and Flora), a legally binding agreement to ensure that the international trade of plants and animals does not threaten the species' survival. CITES went into force in 1975 after 80 countries agreed to the terms. Today, it has grown to include more than 160 countries. This make CITES among the largest conservation agreements in existence.[18]

Another show of international conservation efforts are governments developing economic incentives for local conservation. For example, in 1996, the International Monetary Fund (IMF) and the World Wildlife Fund (WWF) established a program to relieve poor countries of debt. More than 40 countries have benefited by agreeing to direct some of their savings toward environmental programs in the "Debt-for-Nature" swap programs.[19]

It is worth our time to consider the thoughts of two American conservationists and what role we, as individuals, can play in conserving and protecting our world. E. O. Wilson has told us that "Biological Diversity—'biodiversity' in the new parlance—is the key to the maintenance of the world as we know it."[20] Aldo Leopold, the forester who gave Americans the idea of creating a "land ethic," wrote in 1949 that: "Having to squeeze the last drop of utility out of the land has the same desperate finality as having to chop up the furniture to keep warm."[21] All of us have the ability to take part in the struggle to protect our environment and to save our endangered Earth.

ENDNOTES

1   Quammen, David. *Song of the Dodo.* New York: Scribner, 1996, p. 607.

2   Wilson, E. O. *Diversity of Life.* Cambridge, MA: Harvard University Press, 1992, p. 346.

3   Muir, John. *My First Summer in the Sierra.* San Francisco: Sierra Club Books, 1988, p. 110.

4   Press Release. *EPA Newsroom: EPA Issues Designations on Ozone Health Standards.* April 15, 2004. Available online at *http://www.epa.gov/newsroom/.*

5   The Environmental Protection Agency. EPA Newsroom. *May is Allergy Awareness Month.* May 2004. Available online at *http://www.epa.gov/newsroom/allergy_month.htm.*

6   Intergovernmental Panel on Climate Change (IPCC). Third Annual Report, 2001.

7   Turco, Richard P. *Earth Under Siege: From Air Pollution to Global Change.* New York: Oxford University Press, 2002, p. 387.

8   Intergovernmental Panel on Climate Change. *Technical Report V: Climate Change and Biodiversity.* 2002. Full report available online at *http://www.ipcc.ch/pub/tpbiodiv.pdf.*

9   "Roosevelt Quotes." American Museum of Natural History. Available online at *http://www.amnh.org/common/faq/quotes.html.*

10 Wilson, E. O. *Biophilia.* Cambridge, MA: Harvard University Press, 1986, pp. 10–11.

11 Federal Water Pollution Control Act. As amended November 27, 2002. Section 101 (a).

12 Postel, Sandra. *Pillars of Sand.* New York: W. W. Norton & Company, Inc., 1999. p. 6.

13 Hunter, Malcolm L. *Wildlife, Forests, and Forestry: Principles of Managing Forest for Biological Diversity.* Englewood Cliffs, NJ: Prentice-Hall, 1990, p. 4.

14 Dowie, Mark. *Losing Ground: American Environmentalism at the Close of the Twentieth Century.* Cambridge, MA: MIT Press, 1995, p. 113.

15 Leopold, Aldo. *A Sand County Almanac.* New York: Oxford University Press, 1949.

16 Wilson, E. O., ed. *Biodiversity.* Washington, D.C.: National Academies Press, 1988, p. 3.

17 International Whaling Commission Information 2004. Available online at *http://www.iwcoffice.org/commission/iwcmain.htm.*

18 *Discover CITES: What is CITES?* Fact sheet 2004. Available online at *http://www.cites.org/eng/disc/what.shtml.*

19 *Madagascar's Experience with Swapping Debt for the Environment.* World Wildlife Fund Report, 2003. Available online at *http://www.conservationfinance.org/WPC/WPC_documents/ Apps_11_Moye_Paddack_v2.pdf.*

20 Wilson, *Diversity of Life*, p. 15.

21 Leopold.

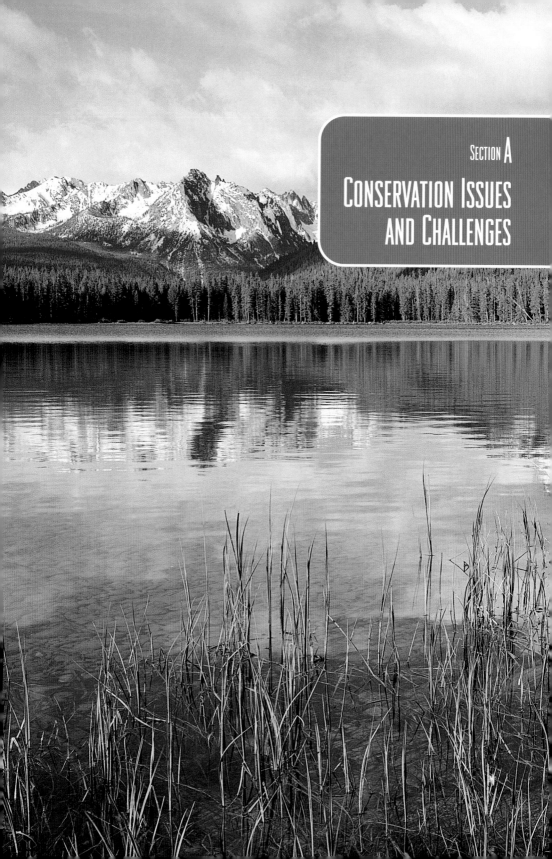

SECTION A
CONSERVATION ISSUES AND CHALLENGES

Does It Matter if Plants and Animals Go Extinct?

It is true that species of plants and animals have been going extinct for millions of years, long before humans started to impact the environment. But, as E. O. Wilson, a Harvard biologist and a Pulitzer Prize—winning author, explains, it has taken tens of millions of years for living things to recover from the past five major extinctions. Wilson states, "These figures should give pause to anyone who believes that what *Homo sapiens* destroy, Nature will redeem. Maybe so, but not within any length of time that has meaning for contemporary humanity."[1]

E. O. Wilson helped develop the concept of biological diversity, or "biodiversity," which became popular in the 1990s as a way to discuss the way living things are organized. Biodiversity includes three levels of organization: ecosystems (for example, rain forests or deserts), species (for example, humans), and genetics (the genes responsible for heredity). Wilson has predicted that if humans keep altering the Earth, we could lose 20% (one-fifth) or more of our plant and animal species by the year 2020.[2] Considering that scientists have, to date, only discovered a small fraction of the 10 to 100 million estimated species on the planet, Wilson's prediction is a serious concern.

The following excerpt is a chapter from Wilson's 2002 book *The Future of Life*. In it, Wilson describes the importance of maintaining biodiversity and the dangers of ignoring the issue. He discusses the diversity of life in our biosphere, which is nothing short of amazing. About 1.5 million species have been identified, and the numbers continue to grow virtually every day. For example, between 1985 and 2001, the number of identified amphibian species grew from 4,003 to 5,282. More than half of the plants and animal species of the world are believed to live in the rain forests, where they are often isolated and hidden from human eyes.

The diversity of life on our planet is a valuable resource for many commercial enterprises, for developing medicines, and for keeping the ecosystems in which we live healthy. Understanding

2

and protecting the diversity of our planet's life also has the potential to answer questions scientists have about evolution and even the possibility of life on other planets. We have the ability to live with the land if we choose to do so. Knowing that it can take tens of millions of years to recover when species go extinct, Wilson warns that we need to develop policies immediately that protect the land and its species while we still have the chance.

—The Editor

1. Wilson, E. O. *The Diversity of Life*. Cambridge, MA: Harvard University Press, 1992, p. 31.

2. Ibid., p. 346.

The Future of Life
by E. O. Wilson

TO THE ENDS OF EARTH

The totality of life, known as the biosphere to scientists and creation to theologians, is a membrane of organisms wrapped around Earth so thin it cannot be seen edgewise from a space shuttle, yet so internally complex that most species composing it remain undiscovered. The membrane is seamless. From Everest's peak to the floor of the Mariana Trench, creatures of one kind or another inhabit virtually every square inch of the planetary surface. They obey the fundamental principle of biological geography, that wherever there is liquid water, organic molecules, and an energy source, there is life. Given the near-universality of organic materials and energy of some kind or other, water is the deciding element on planet Earth. It may be no more than a transient film on grains of sand, it may never see sunlight, it may be boiling hot or supercooled, but there will be some kind of organism living in or upon it. Even if nothing alive is visible to the naked eye, single cells of microorganisms will be growing and reproducing there, or at least dormant and awaiting the arrival of liquid water to kick them back into activity.

An extreme example is the McMurdo Dry Valleys of Antarctica, whose soils are the coldest, driest, and most nutritionally deficient in the world. On first inspection the habitat seems as sterile as a cabinet of autoclaved glassware. In 1903, Robert F. Scott, the first to explore the region, wrote, "We have seen no living thing, not even a moss or lichen; all that we did find, far inland among the moraine heaps, was the skeleton of a Weddell seal, and how that came there is beyond guessing." On all of Earth the McMurdo Dry Valleys most resemble the rubbled plains of Mars.

But the trained eye, aided by a microscope, sees otherwise. In the parched streambeds live twenty species of photosynthetic bacteria, a comparable variety of mostly single-celled algae, and an array of microscopic invertebrate animals that feed on these primary producers. All depend on the summer flow of glacial and icefield meltwater for their annual spurts of growth. Because the paths of the streams change over time, some of the populations are stranded and forced to wait for years, perhaps centuries, for the renewed flush of meltwater. In the even more brutal conditions on bare land away from the stream channels live sparse assemblages of microbes and fungi together with rotifers, bear animalcules, mites, and springtails feeding on them. At the top of this rarefied food web are four species of nematode worms, each specialized to consume different species in the rest of the flora and fauna. With the mites and springtails they are also the largest of the animals, McMurdo's equivalent of elephants and tigers, yet all but invisible to the naked eye.

The McMurdo Dry Valley's organisms are what scientists call extremophiles, species adapted to live at the edge of biological tolerance. Many populate the environmental ends of Earth, in places that seem uninhabitable to gigantic, fragile animals like ourselves. They constitute, to take a second example, the "gardens" of the Antarctic sea ice. The thick floes, which blanket millions of square miles of ocean water around the continent much of the year, seem forbiddingly hostile to life. But they are riddled with channels of slushy brine in which single-celled algae flourish year-round, assimilating the carbon dioxide, phosphates, and other nutrients that work up from the ocean below. The garden photosynthesis is driven by energy from sunlight penetrating the translucent matrix. As the ice melts and erodes during the polar summer, the algae sink into the water below, where they are consumed by copepods and krill. These tiny crustaceans in turn are the prey of fish whose blood is kept liquid by biochemical antifreezes.

The ultimate extremophiles are certain specialized microbes, including bacteria and their superficially similar but genetically very different relatives the archaeans. (To take a necessary digression: biologists now recognize three domains of life on the basis of DNA sequences and cell structure. They are the Bacteria, which are the conventionally recognized microbes; the Archaea, the other microbes; and the Eukarya, which include the single-celled protists or "protozoans," the fungi, and all of the animals, including us. Bacteria and archaeans are more primitive than other organisms in cell structure: they lack membranes around their nuclei as well as organelles such as chloroplasts and mitochondria.) Some specialized species of bacteria and archaeans live in the walls of volcanic hydrothermal vents on the ocean floor, where they multiply in water close to or above the boiling point. A bacterium found there, *Pyrolobus fumarii,* is the reigning world champion among the hyperthermophiles, or lovers of extreme heat. It can reproduce at 2–35°F [-16.7–1.7°C], does best at 221°F [105°C], and stops growing when the temperature drops to a chilly 194°F [90°C]. This extraordinary feat has prompted microbiologists to inquire whether even more advanced, ultrathermophiles exist, occupying geothermal waters at 400°F or even higher. Watery environments with temperatures that hot exist. The submarine spumes close to the *Pyrolobus fumarii* bacterial colonies reach 660°F [349°C]. The absolute upper limit of life as a whole, bacteria and archaeans included, is thought to be about 300°F [149°C], at which point organisms cannot sustain the integrity of DNA and the proteins on which known forms of life depend. But until the search for ultrathermophiles, as opposed to mere hyperthermophiles, is exhausted, no one can say for certain that these intrinsic limits actually exist.

During more than three billion years of evolution, the bacteria and archaeans have pushed the boundaries in other dimensions of physiological adaptation. One species, an acid lover (acidophile), flourishes in the hot sulfur springs of Yellowstone National Park. At the opposite end of the pH scale, alkaliphiles occupy carbonate-laden soda lakes around the world. Halophiles are specialized for life in saturated salt lakes and salt evaporation ponds. Others, the barophiles (pressure lovers), colonize the floor of the deepest reaches of the ocean. In 1996, Japanese scientists used a small unmanned submersible to retrieve bottom mud from the Challenger Deep of the Mariana Trench, which at 35,750 feet [10,897 meters] is the lowest point of the world's oceans. In the samples they discovered hundreds of species of bacteria, archaeans, and fungi. Transferred to the laboratory, some of the bacteria were able to grow at the pressure found in the Challenger Deep, which is a thousand times greater than that near the ocean surface.

The outer reach of physiological resilience of any kind may have been attained by *Deinococcus radiodurans*, a bacterium that can live through radiation so intense the glass of a Pyrex beaker holding them is cooked to a discolored and fragile state. A human being exposed to 1,000 rads of radiation energy, a dose delivered in the atomic explosions at Hiroshima and Nagasaki, dies within one or two weeks. At 1,000 times this amount, 1 million rads, the growth of the *Deinococcus* is slowed, but all the bacteria still survive. At 1.75 million rads, 37 percent make it through, and even at 3 million rads a very small number still endure. The secret of this superbug is its extraordinary ability to repair broken DNA. All organisms have an enzyme that can replace chromosome parts that have been shorn off, whether by radiation, chemical insult, or accident. The more conventional bacterium *Escherichia coli*, a dominant inhabitant of the human gut, can repair two or three breaks at one time. The superbug can manage five hundred breaks. The special molecular techniques it uses remain unknown.

Deinococcus radiodurans and its close relatives are not just extremophiles but ultimate generalists and world travelers, having been found, for example, in llama feces, Antarctic rocks, the tissue of Atlantic haddock, and a can of ground pork and beef irradiated by scientists in Oregon. They join a select group, also including cyanobacteria of the genus *Chroococcidiopsis*, that thrive where very few other organisms venture. They are Earth's outcast nomads, looking for life in all the worst places.

By virtue of their marginality, the superbugs are also candidates for space travel. Microbiologists have begun to ask whether the hardiest among them might drift away from Earth, propelled by stratospheric winds into the void, eventually to settle alive on Mars. Conversely, indigenous microbes from Mars (or beyond) might have colonized Earth. Such is the theory of the origin of life called panspermia, once ridiculed but now an undeniable possibility.

The superbugs have also given a new shot of hope to exobiologists, scientists who look for evidences of life on other worlds. Another stimulus is the newly revealed existence of SLIMEs (subsurface lithoautotrophic microbial ecosystems), unique assemblages of bacteria and fungi that occupy pores in the interlocking mineral grains of igneous rock beneath Earth's surface. Thriving to a depth of up to two miles or more, they obtain their energy from inorganic chemicals. Because they do not require organic particles that filter down from conventional plants and animals whose ultimate energy is from sunlight, the SLIMEs are wholly independent of life on the surface. Consequently, even if all of life as we know it were somehow extinguished, these microscopic troglodytes would carry on. Given enough time, a billion years perhaps, they would likely evolve new forms able to colonize the surface and resynthesize the precatastrophe world run by photosynthesis.

The major significance of the SLIMEs for exobiology is the heightened possibility they suggest of life on other planets and Mars in particular. SLIMEs, or their extraterrestrial equivalent, might live deep within the red planet. During its early, aqueous period Mars had rivers, lakes, and perhaps time to evolve its own surface organisms. According to one recent estimate, there was enough water to cover the entire Martian surface to a depth of five hundred meters. Some, perhaps most, of the water may still exist in permafrost, surface ice covered by the dust we now see from our landers—or, far below the surface, in liquid form. How far below? Physicists believe there is enough heat inside Mars to liquefy water. It comes from a combination of decaying radioactive minerals, some gravitational heat remaining from the original assembly of the planet out of smaller cosmic fragments, and gravitational energy from the sinking of heavier elements and rise of lighter ones. A recent model of the combined effects suggests that the temperature of Mars increases with depth in the upper crustal layers at a rate of 6°F [-14.4°C] per mile. As a consequence, water could be liquid at eighteen miles beneath the surface. But some water may well up occasionally from the aquifers. In 2000, high-resolution scans by an orbiting satellite revealed the presence of gullies that may have been cut by running streams in the last few centuries or even decades. If Martian life did arise on the planet, or arrived in space particles from Earth, it must include extremophiles, some of which are (or were) ecologically independent single-celled organisms able to persist in or beneath the permafrost.

An equal contender for extraterrestrial life in the solar system is Europa, the second moon out (after Io) of Jupiter. Europa is ice-covered, and long cracks and filled-in meteorite craters on its surface suggest there is an ocean of brine or slurried ice beneath the surface. The evidence is consistent with the likelihood of persistent interior heat in Europa caused by its gravitational tug of war with nearby Jupiter, Io, and Callisto. The main ice crust may be six miles thick, but crisscrossed with far thinner regions on top of upwelling liquid water, thin enough in fact to create slabs that move like icebergs. Do SLIME-like autotrophs float and swim in the Europan Ocean beneath? To planetary scientists and biologists the odds appear good enough to have a look, and practical enough to test—if we can soft-land probes on the upwelling surface cracks and drill through the ice skims that cover them. A second, although less promising, candidate is Callisto, the most distant of Jupiter's larger moons, which may have an ice crust about sixty miles thick and an underlying salt ocean up to twelve miles deep. On Earth, the closest approach to the putative oceans of Europa and Callisto is Antarctica's Lake Vostok. About the size of Lake Ontario, with depths exceeding 1,500 feet, Vostok is located under two miles of the East Antarctic Ice Sheet in the remotest part of the continent. It is at least one million years old, wholly dark, under immense pressure, and fully isolated from other ecosystems. If any environment on Earth is sterile, it should be Lake Vostok. Yet this hidden world contains organisms. Scientists have recently drilled through the glacial ice to the six-hundred-foot bottom layer adjacent to the lake. The lowest core samples contained a sparse diversity of bacteria and fungi almost certainly derived from the underlying water. The drill will not be pushed on down into the liquid water. To do so would contaminate one of the last remaining pristine habitats on Earth. The Vostok operation, while telling us very little as yet about the possibility of extraterrestrial life, is a precursor of similar probes likely to be conducted during this century on Mars and the Jovian moons Europa and Callisto.

Suppose that autotrophs parallel to those on Earth originated without benefit of sunlight. Could they have also given rise in the stygian darkness to animals of some kind? The image leaps to mind of crustacean-like species filtering the microbes and larger, fishlike animals hunting the crustaceoids. A recent discovery on planet Earth suggests that such independent evolution of complex life forms can occur. Romania's Movile Cave was sealed off from the outside more than 5.5 million years ago. During that time it evidently received oxygen through minute cracks in the overlying rocks, but no organic material from the sunlight-driven flora and fauna in the world above. Although the peculiar life forms of most caves around the world draw at least part of their energy from the outside, this is evidently not the case for the Movile Cave and may never have been. The energy base is the autotrophic bacteria, which metabolize hydrogen sulfide from the rocks. Feeding on them and each other are no fewer than forty-eight species of animals, of which thirty-three proved new to science when the cave was explored. The microbe grazers, equivalent to plant eaters on the outside, include pill bugs, springtails, millipedes, and bristle-tails. Among the carnivores that hunt the microbe grazers are pseudoscorpions, centipedes, and spiders. These more complex organisms are descended from ancestors that entered before the cave was sealed. A second example of an independent stygian system, although not entirely closed to the outside, is Cueva de Villa Luz (Cave of the Lighted House), on the edge of the Chiapas highlands in Tabasco, southern Mexico. Here too the energy base is metabolism by the autotrophic bacteria. Forming layers over the inner cave walls, they subsist on hydrogen sulfide and support a multifarious swarm of small animals.

Studies of the distribution of life have revealed several fundamental patterns in the way species proliferate and are fitted together in Earth's far-flung ecosystems. The first, the most elementary, is that bacteria and archaeans occur every-where there is life of any kind, whether on the surface or deep beneath it. The second is that, if there is even the smallest space through which to wriggle or swim, tiny protists and invertebrates invade and proceed to prey on the microbes and one another. The third principle is that the more space avail-able, up to and including the largest ecosystems such as grasslands and oceans, the larger are the largest animals living in them. And finally, the greatest diversity of life, as measured by the number of species, occurs in habitats with the most year-round solar energy, the widest exposure of ice-free terrain, the most varied terrain, and the greatest climatic stability across long stretches of time. Thus the equatorial rainforests of the Asian, African, and South American continents possess by far the largest number of plant and animal species.

Regardless of its magnitude, biodiversity (short for biological diversity) is everywhere organized into three levels. At the top are the ecosystems, such as rainforests, coral reefs, and lakes. Next are the species, composed of the organisms in the ecosystems, from algae and swallowtail butterflies to moray eels and people. At the bottom are the variety of genes making up the heredity of individuals that compose each of the species.

Every species is bound to its community in the unique manner by which it variously consumes, is consumed, competes, and cooperates with other species. It also indirectly affects the community in the way it alters the soil, water, and air. The ecologist sees the whole as a network of energy and material continuously flowing into the community from the surrounding physical environment, and back out, and then on round to create the perpetual ecosystem cycles on which our own existence depends.

It is easy to visualize an ecosystem, especially if it is as physically discrete as, say, a marsh or an alpine meadow. But does its dynamical network of organisms, materials, and energy link it to other ecosystems? In 1972 the British inventor and scientist James E. Lovelock said that, in fact, it is tied to the entire biosphere, which can be thought of as a kind of super-organism that surrounds the planet. This singular entity he called Gaia, after Gaea, or Ge, a vaguely personal goddess of early Greece, giver of dreams, divine personification of Earth, and object of the cult of Earth, as well as mother of the seas, the mountains, and the twelve Titans—in other words, *big*. There is considerable merit in looking at life in this grand holistic manner. Alone among the solar planets, Earth's physical environment is held by its organisms in a delicate equilibrium utterly different from what would be the case in their absence. There is plenty of evidence that even some individual species have a measurable global impact. In the most notable example, the oceanic phytoplankton, composed of microscopic, photosynthesizing bacteria, archaeans, and algae, is a major player in the control of the world climate. Dimethylsulfide generated by the algae alone is believed to be an important factor in the regulation of cloud formation.

The concept of the biosphere as Gaia has two versions: strong and weak. The strong version holds that the biosphere is a true superorganism, with each of the species in it optimized to stabilize the environment and benefit from balance in the entire system, like cells of the body or workers of an ant colony. This is a lovely metaphor, with a kernel of truth, providing the idea of superorganism is broadened enough. The strong version, however, is generally rejected by biologists, including Lovelock himself, as a working principle. The weak version, on the other hand, which holds that some species exercise widespread and even global influence, is well substantiated. Its acceptance has stimulated important new programs of research.

Looking at the totality of life, the POET asks, Who are Gaia's children?

The ECOLOGIST responds, They are the species. We must know the role each one plays in the whole in order to manage Earth wisely.

The SYSTEMATIST adds, Then let's get started. How many species exist? Where are they in the world? Who are their genetic kin?

Systematists, the biologists who specialize in classification, favor the species as the unit by which to measure biodiversity. They build on the system of classification invented in the mid-1700s by the Swedish naturalist Carolus Linnaeus. In the Linnaean system each species is given a two-part Latinized name such as *Canis lupus*, for the gray wolf, with *lupus* being the species and *Canis* the genus of wolves and dogs. Similarly, all of humanity composes the species *Homo sapiens*. Today there is only one member of our very distinctive genus, but as recently as 27,000 years ago there was also *Homo neanderthalensis*, the Neanderthal people who preceded *Homo sapiens* in glacier-bound Europe.

The species is the base of the entire Linnaean system and the unit by which biologists traditionally visualize the span of life. The higher categories from genus to domain are simply the means by which the degrees of similarity are subjectively assayed and roughly described. When we say *Homo neanderthalensis*, we mean a species close to *Homo sapiens*; when we say *Australopithecus africanus*, to designate one of the ancestral man-apes, we mean a creature different enough from the species of *Homo* to be placed in another genus, *Australopithecus*. And when we assert that all three of the species composing two genera are hominids, we mean they are close enough to one another to be classified as members of the same family, the Hominidae. The closest living relations of the Hominidae are the common chimpanzee, *Pan troglodytes*, and the pygmy chimpanzee, or bonobo, *Pan paniscus*. They are similar enough to each other, and share sufficiently close common ancestry, to be put in the same genus, *Pan*. And both are different enough from the hominids, with distant enough common ancestry, to constitute not only a distinct genus but a separate family, the Pongidae. The Pongidae also includes a second genus for the orangutan and a third for the two species of gorillas.

And thus in visualizing life we travel nomenclaturally outward through the gossamer pavilions of Earth's biodiversity. The principles of higher classification are very easy to grasp, once you get used to the Latinized names. The Linnaean system builds up hierarchically to the higher categories of biodiversity by the same basic principles used to organize ground combat troops, proceeding from squads to platoons to companies to divisions to corps to armies. Returning to the gray wolf, its genus *Canis*, the common dogs and wolves, are placed into the family Canidae with other genera that hold the species of coyotes and foxes. Families are grouped into orders; the order Carnivora are all the canids plus the families respectively of bears, cats, weasels, raccoons, and hyenas. Orders are clustered into classes, with the class Mammalia composed of the carnivores and all other mammals, and classes are clustered into phyla, in this particular progression the phylum Chordata, which includes mammals and all other vertebrates as well as the vertebra-less lancelets and sea squirts. Thence phyla into kingdoms (Bacteria, Archaea, Protista, Fungi, Animalia, Plantae); and finally, at the summit, encompassing everything, there are the three great domains of life on Earth, the Bacteria, the Archaea, and the Eukarya, the last comprising the protistans (also called protozoans), fungi, animals, and plants.

But always, the real units that can be seen and counted as corporeal objects are the species. Like troops in the field, they are present and waiting to be counted, regardless of how we arbitrarily group and name them. How many species are there in the world? Somewhere between 1.5 and 1.8 million have been discovered and given a formal scientific name. No one has yet made an exact count from the taxonomic literature published over the past 250 years. We know this much, however: the roster, whatever its length, is but a mere beginning. Estimates of the true number of living species range, according to the method used, from 3.6 million to 100 million or more. The median of the estimates is a little over 10 million, but few experts would risk their reputations by insisting on this figure or any other, even to the nearest million.

The truth is that we have only begun to explore life on Earth. How little we know is epitomized by bacteria of the genus *Prochlorococcus*, arguably the most abundant organisms on the planet and responsible for a large part of the organic production of the ocean—yet unknown to science until 1988. *Prochlorococcus* cells float passively in open water at 70,000 to 200,000 per milliliter, multiplying with energy captured from sunlight. Their extremely small size is what makes them so elusive. They belong to a special group called picoplankton, forms even smaller than conventional bacteria and barely visible even at the highest optical magnification.

The blue ocean teems with other novel and little-known bacteria, archaeans, and protozoans. When researchers began to focus on them in the 1990s, they discovered that these organisms are vastly more abundant and diverse than anyone had previously imagined. Much of this miniature world exists in and around previously unseen dark matter, composed of wispy aggregates of colloids, cell fragments, and polymers that range in diameter from billionths to hundredths of a meter. Some of the material contains "hot spots" of nutrients that attract scavenger bacteria and their tiny bacterial and protozoan predators. The ocean we peer into, seemingly clear with only an occasional fish and invertebrate passing beneath, is not the ocean we thought. The visible organisms are just the tip of a vast biomass pyramid.

Among the multicellular organisms of Earth in all environments, the smallest species are also the least known. Of the fungi, which are nearly as ubiquitous as the microbes, 69,000 species have been identified and named, but as many as 1.6 million are thought to exist. Of the nematode worms, making up four of every five animals on Earth and the most widely distributed, 15,000 species are known, but millions more may await discovery.

During the molecular revolution in biology, which spanned the second half of the twentieth century, systematics was judged to be a largely outdated discipline. It was pushed aside and kept on minimal rations. Now the renewal of the Linnaean enterprise is seen as high adventure; systematics has returned to the center of the action in biology. The reasons for the renaissance are multiple. Molecular biology has provided systematics the tools to speed the discovery of microscopic organisms. New techniques are now available in genetics and mathematical tree theory to trace the evolution of life in a swift and convincing manner. All this has happened just in time. The global environmental crisis gives urgency to the full and exact mapping of all biological diversity.

One of the open frontiers in biodiversity exploration is the floor of the ocean, which from surf to abyss covers 70 percent of Earth's surface. All of the thirty-six known animal phyla, the highest-ranking and most inclusive groups in the taxonomic hierarchy, occur there, as opposed to only ten on the land. Among the most familiar are the Arthropoda, or the insects, crustaceans, spiders, and their sundry relations; and the Mollusca, comprising the snails, mussels, and octopuses. Amazingly, two marine phyla have been discovered during the past thirty years: the Loricifera, miniature bullet-shaped organisms with a girdlelike band around their middle, described for the first time in 1983; and the Cycliophora, plump symbiotic forms that attach themselves to the mouths of lobsters and filter out food particles left over from their hosts' meals, described in 1996. Swarming around the loriciferans and cycliophorans, and deep into the soil of shallow marine waters, are other Alice-in-Wonderland creatures, the meiofauna, most of them barely visible to the naked eye. The strange creatures include gastrotrichs, gnathostomulids, kinorhynchs, tardigrades, chaetognaths, placozoans, and orthonectids, along with nematodes and worm-shaped ciliate protozoans. They can be found in buckets of sand drawn from the intertidal surf and offshore shallow water around the world. So, for those seeking a new form of recreation, plan a day at the nearest beach. Take an umbrella, bucket, trowel, microscope, and illustrated textbook on invertebrate zoology. Don't build sand castles but explore, and as you enjoy this watery microcosm keep in mind what the great nineteenth-century physicist Michael Faraday correctly said, that nothing in this world is too wonderful to be true.

Even the most familiar small organisms are less studied than might be guessed. About ten thousand species of ants are known and named, but that number may double when tropical regions are more fully explored. While recently conducting a study of *Pheidole*, one of the world's two largest ant genera, I uncovered 341 new species, more than doubling the number in the genus and increasing the entire known fauna of ants in the Western Hemisphere by 10 percent. As my monograph went to press in 2001, additional new species were still pouring in, mostly from fellow entomologists collecting in the tropics.

You will recognize this frequent image in popular entertainment: a scientist discovers a new species of animal or plant (perhaps after an arduous journey up a tributary of the Orinoco). His team at base camp celebrates, opening a bottle of champagne, and radios the news to the home institution. The truth, I assure you, is almost always different. The small number of scientists expert in the classification of each of the most diverse groups, from bacteria to fungi and insects, are inundated with new species almost to the breaking point. Working mostly alone, they try desperately to keep their collections in order while eking out enough time to publish accounts of a small fraction of the novelties sent to them for identification.

Even the flowering plants, traditionally a favorite of field biologists, retain large pockets of unexamined diversity. About 272,000 species have been described worldwide, but the true number is likely to be 300,000 or more. Each year about 2,000 new species are added to the world list published in botany's standard reference work, the *Index Kewensis*. Even the relatively well-curried United States and Canada continue to yield about 60 new species annually. Some experts believe that as much as 5 percent of the North American flora await discovery, including 300 or more species and races in the biologically rich state of California alone. The novelties are usually rare but not necessarily shy and inconspicuous. Some, like the recently described Shasta snow-wreath (*Neviusia cliftonii*), are flamboyant enough to serve as ornamentals. Many grow in plain sight. A member of the lily family, *Calochortus tiburonensis*, first described in 1972, grows just ten miles from downtown San Francisco. In 1982, a twenty-one-year-old amateur collector, James Morefield, discovered the brand-new leather flower, *Clematis morefieldii*, on the outskirts of Huntsville, Alabama.

Ever deeper rounds of zoological exploration, driven by a sense of urgency over vanishing environments, have revealed surprising numbers of new vertebrates, many of which are placed on the endangered list as soon as they are discovered.

The global number of amphibian species, including frogs, toads, salamanders, and the less familiar tropical caecilians, grew between 1985 and 2001 by one third, from 4,003 to 5,282. There can be little doubt that in time it will pass 6,000.

The discovery of new mammals has also continued at a rapid pace. Collectors, by journeying to remote tropical regions and concentrating on small elusive forms such as tenrecs and shrews, have increased the global number in the last two decades from about 4,000 to 5,000. The record for rapid discovery during the past half-century was set by James L. Patton in July 1996. With just three weeks' effort in the central Andes of Colombia, he discovered 6 new species—four mice, a shrew, and a marsupial. Even primates, including apes, monkeys, and lemurs, the most sought of all mammals in the field, are yielding novelties. In the 1990s alone Russell Mittermeier and his colleagues managed to add 9 new species to the 275 previously known. Mittermeier, whose searches take him to tropical forests around the world, estimates that at least another hundred species of primates await discovery.

New land mammals of large size are a rarity, but even a few of them continue to turn up. Perhaps the most surprising find in recent memory was the discovery during the mid-1990s of not one but four big animals in the Annamite Mountains between Vietnam and Laos. Included are a striped hare; a seventy-five-pound barking deer, or giant muntjac; and a smaller, thirty-five-pound barking deer. But most astonishing is the two-hundred-pound cowlike animal called saola, or "spindlehorn," by the local people and Vu Quang bovid by zoologists. It was the first land vertebrate of this size to be discovered for more than fifty years. The saola is not closely related to any other known ungulate mammal. It has been placed in a genus of its own, *Pseudoryx*, meaning false oryx, in reference to its superficial resemblance to the true oryx, a large African antelope. Only a few hundred saola are thought to exist. Their numbers are probably dwindling fast from native hunting and the clearing of the forests in which they live. No scientist has yet seen one in the wild, but in 1998 a photograph was captured by a pressure-released trap camera. And for a short time, before she died, a female brought in by Hmong hunters was kept in the zoo at Lak Xao, Laos.

For centuries, birds have been the most pursued and best known of all animals, but here again new species are still coming to light at a steady pace. From 1920 to 1934, the golden age of ornithological field research, an average of about ten subsequently authenticated species were described each year. The number dropped to between two and three and remained steady thereafter into the 1990s. By the end of the century, approximately ten thousand valid species were securely established in the world register. Then, an unexpected revolution in field studies opened the census to a flood of new candidate species. Experts had come to recognize the possible existence of large numbers of sibling species-populations closely resembling one another in anatomical traits traditionally used in taxonomy, such as size, plumage, and bill shape, yet differing strongly in other, equally important traits discoverable only in the field, such as habitat preference and mating call. The fundamental criterion used to separate species of birds, as well as most other kinds of animals, is that provided by the biological species concept: populations belong to different species if they are incapable of interbreeding freely under natural conditions. As field studies have increased in sophistication, more such genetically isolated populations have come to light. Old species recently subdivided into multiple species include the familiar *Phylloscopus*, leaf warblers, of Europe and Asia and, more controversially, the crossbills of North America. An important new analytic method is song playback, in which ornithologists record the songs of one population and play them in the presence of another population. If the birds show little interest in each other's songs, they can be reasonably assumed to represent different species, because they would presumably not interbreed if they met in nature. The playback method makes possible for the first time the evaluation not only of populations occupying the same range but also those living apart and classified as geographic races, or subspecies. It is not out of the question that the number of validated living bird species will eventually double, to twenty thousand.

More than half the plant and animal species of the world are believed to occur in the tropical rainforests. From these natural greenhouses, which occupy the opposite end of the biodiversity scale from the McMurdo Dry Valleys, many world records of biodiversity have been reported: 425 kinds of trees in a single hectare (2.5 acres) of Brazil's Atlantic Forest, for example, and 1,300 butterfly species from a corner of Peru's Manu National Park. Both numbers are ten times greater than those from comparable sites in Europe and North America. The record for ants is 365 species from 10 hectares (25 acres) in a forest tract of the upper Peruvian Amazon. I have identified 43 species from the canopy of a single tree in the same region, approximately equal to the ant fauna of all the British Isles.

These impressive censuses do not exclude a comparable richness of some groups of organisms in other major environments of the world. A single coral head in Indonesia can harbor hundreds of species of crustaceans, polychaete worms, and other invertebrates, plus a fish or two. Twenty-eight kinds of vines and herbaceous plants have been found growing on a giant *Podocarpus* yellowwood conifer in the temperate rainforest of New Zealand, setting the world record for vascular epiphytes on a single tree. As many as two hundred species of mites, diminutive spiderlike creatures, teem in a single square meter of some hardwood forests of North America. In the same spot a gram of soil—a pinch held between thumb and forefinger—contains thousands of species of bacteria. A few are actively multiplying, but most are dormant, each awaiting the special combination of nutrients, moisture, aridity, and temperature to which its particular strain is adapted.

You do not have to visit distant places, or even rise from your seat, to experience the luxuriance of biodiversity. You yourself are a rainforest of a kind. There is a good chance that tiny spiderlike mites build nests at the base of your eyelashes.

Fungal spores and hyphae on your toenails await the right conditions to sprout a Lilliputian forest. The vast majority of the cells in your body are not your own; they belong to bacterial and other microorganismic species. More than four hundred such microbial species make their home in your mouth. But rest easy: the bulk of protoplasm you carry around is still human, because microbial cells are so small. Every time you scuff earth or splash mud puddles with your shoes, bacteria, and who knows what else, that are still unknown to science settle on them.

Such is the biospheric membrane that covers Earth, and you and me. It is the miracle we have been given. And our tragedy, because a large part of it is being lost forever before we learn what it is and the best means by which it can be savored and used.

How Did the Environmental Movement Get Started in Our Country?

The belief that we should value and protect our land, our water, and our wetlands is the basis of conservation. But we must recognize that different people view natural resources in very different ways. Some see undisturbed nature as most precious, while others see more value in the Earth's commercial potential. Americans have argued for hundreds of years about what "value" means when it comes to nature. Throughout this lengthy debate, animals have gone extinct, rivers have caught on fire, and wetlands have been turned into parking lots. It has become clear to many people that a balance has to be found between using natural resources such as gas, trees, and water, and protecting the environment.

Philip Shabecoff is a noted environmental journalist. He worked as a reporter for *The New York Times* for 32 years, and was the founder and publisher of *Greenwire*, an environmental news daily. He also is the author of several books, including *A Fierce Green Fire* and *A New Name for Peace*. In his book *Earth Rising*, from which the following excerpt is taken, Shabecoff explores the development of the environmental movement in the United States. The ripples of the "first wave" of the movement began with such visionaries as Ralph Waldo Emerson and Henry David Thoreau over 150 years ago. But the real impetus of the early environmental movement can be credited to the thoughts and actions of three men who lived at the beginning of the 20th century: John Muir, Theodore Roosevelt, and Gifford Pinchot. John Muir was a naturalist and explorer who believed nature should be preserved for its own sake. Roosevelt, the 26th U.S. president, and Pinchot, who served as chief of the U.S. Division of Forestry, believed that our resources should be managed to meet the present needs of the people, but they insisted that natural assets must be preserved for future generations.

During the 1960s and 1970s, an increasing amount of scientific evidence came to light showing that pollution was damaging the Earth and people's health. The focus of environmentalists shifted to concerns about pollution and toxic waste. Rachel Carson's 1962 book *Silent Spring*, the nation's first Earth Day in 1970, and the creation of the U.S. Environmental Protection Agency (EPA), also in 1970, were all part of this "second wave" of the environmental movement. In the 1990s, after President Ronald Reagan's attempts to reverse some environmental protection laws, what has been called "the third wave" of the movement began. Environmental organizations began to work with industry, the public, and Congress to deal with pollution issues.

The American environmental movement has developed over many years and includes many diverse groups and ways of thinking. And in this diversity, one hopes, lies its strength. The challenge of the yet-to-be-formed "fourth wave," Shabecoff notes, is that it must be "sophisticated, visionary, and aggressive" enough to deal with all the environmental problems facing both the planet and all of its inhabitants.

—The Editor

"The Story Until Now"
by Philip Shabecoff

About a century ago, in the middle of a thunderstorm high in the Sierra Nevada, a gaunt, bearded man climbed to the top of a wildly swaying evergreen tree, in order, he later explained, to enjoy riding the wind.

A few years later, the first head of the USDA [U.S. Department of Agriculture] Forest Service, a patrician, European-trained forester, was riding his horse through Rock Creek Park in Washington, D.C., when he had a sudden flash of insight. The health and vitality of the nation, he realized, depended on the health and vitality of the country's natural resources.

The White House, a few blocks away, was then occupied by a president who liked to shoot big game animals but who venerated wilderness and had conceived the idea, radical for the time, that the country's public forests, lands, and waters should be used for the benefit of all the American people, not just to increase the wealth of a few grasping robber barons.

These three charismatic, idiosyncratic contemporaries of a hundred years ago—John Muir, Gifford Pinchot, and Theodore Roosevelt—presided at the birth of one of the great cultural innovations of the 20th century: the modern environmental movement in the United States.

Over the course of the century, the movement grew and changed and achieved results far beyond the dreams of even those three visionaries. Many of their goals and dreams were realized as laws and institutions, in cleaner air and water, and in protected parks and forests, wildlife and wilderness areas. Over time, many, if not most, Americans, informed and prodded by the environmentalists, came to understand and integrate their values.

By century's end, however, it was an open question whether the environmental movement had reached the limits of its effectiveness. The problems had become much bigger, more complex and intractable, the solutions less clear. The forces arrayed against the environmentalists were stronger and more aggressive and sophisticated. The movement as a whole seemed increasingly subdued, less sure of its goals and how to accomplish them.

The roots of American environmentalism were planted well before the 19th century and are deeply embedded in the nation's history. Since colonial times, there were those who perceived—and some who lamented—the dramatic transformation of a pristine continent as a result of European migration, European technology, European economics, and European values. The great sweep of settlement across North America and the powerful tools and voracious demand for resources created by the industrial revolution profoundly changed the land and its people and did so with astonishing speed.

Some 150 years ago, transcendentalist Henry David Thoreau, sitting in his tiny cabin on Walden Pond in Concord, Massachusetts, was already mourning the loss of the wilderness and the debilitating effect of industrialism on the human spirit. In 1864, another New Englander, George Perkins Marsh, warned in his great work *Man and Nature; or, Physical Geography as Modified by Human Action*[1] that human activity could permanently damage the earth. The protection of Yosemite Valley by the state of California in that same year and the creation of Yellowstone National Park by Congress in 1872 were signals that the nation recognized the loss of its natural heritage and the need to preserve some portion of it for future generations. Across the young country, citizens in a few communities, troubled by the effects of sewage, unbreathable air, mining waste, or loss of forests and watersheds, organized locally to try to protect their surroundings and their health.

But American environmentalism—or conservation, to give it its birth name—was essentially a child of the 20th century, and Muir, Pinchot, and Roosevelt were indispensable in its creation.

For Pinchot and Roosevelt, conservation was a merger of science and democracy. Public lands and resources, they insisted, should be scientifically managed so that they would continue to serve the needs of all Americans, including future generations. Both men were sensible of the aesthetic and spiritual values of nature. But they preached what historian Samuel P. Hays called "the gospel of efficiency," which valued nature for its contribution to the public weal rather than for its beauty and other intrinsic qualities. They helped place huge areas of the public domain under permanent federal protection in the National Forest System and the National Wildlife Refuge System. Their efforts assured the environment of a permanent place on the nation's political agenda.

John Muir, a naturalist, writer, and mystic, introduced a different theme into the opening chapter of modern environmentalism. Imbued with a transcendental reverence for nature, Muir eloquently and passionately insisted that the natural world be preserved for its own sake as well as for humanity's. Everything in the universe, he maintained, is "hitched" to everything else, and humans tampering with any one part were interfering with the great cosmic plan. Muir also was a founder of the Sierra Club, the first of the major citizens' organizations that would increasingly rally to the defense of the environment over the course of the century. Among the other private conservation organizations founded in the first half of the 20th century and still in operation are the National Audubon Society, the National Parks and Conservation Association, the Izaak Walton League of America, The Wilderness Society, the National Wildlife Federation, Ducks Unlimited, and Defenders of Wildlife.

The early conservation movement, the "first wave" of environmentalism, was somewhat elitist. Its cadre and adherents tended to be affluent white Protestant males eager to protect wildlife for hunting and fishing and to preserve open space for aesthetics and recreation. Several early national conservation groups, including the Sierra Club, were for a time largely social organizations that existed to provide outdoor excursions for their members.[2]

Over the course of the century, however, rapid demographic, economic, and industrial growth created increasingly difficult, dangerous, and challenging risks to the environment, risks that could not be addressed by the tools of traditional conservation. The disappearance of wildlife, the fouling of the country's waters, the darkening of its skies from pollution, the loss of soil from erosion—especially during the dust bowl years—the onset of urban sprawl and disappearing farmland, and the introduction of hazardous chemicals and other substances into the air, water, and land by new industrial and agricultural processes grew as nagging concerns in the national consciousness.

But for much of the century, environmental dangers remained at the periphery of the nation's affairs. Public health officials and a few social activists tried to do something about the effects of environmental degradation on communities and workers. These efforts, however, were regarded as something apart from the nascent environmental movement.[3] Preoccupied by two world wars and the hardships of the Great Depression, Americans paid little attention to the effects of a ballooning population and rapid industrial growth on the natural world and on themselves. In the years after World War II, citizens were engulfed in a rising tide of materialism and a careless optimism tempered only by the cold war and the threat of nuclear annihilation.

In those same postwar years, however, powerful new technologies and explosive economic expansion created environmental pressures that could not be ignored. The country's quickly growing automotive fleet, powered by high-combustion engines, spread across the land on the new Interstate Highway System, pouring pollution into the air. Smoke from coal-fired power plants thickened the witches' brew of contaminants in the air, helping to produce a noxious haze that darkened the air in cities and dropped acid rain on streams, lakes, and forests. Nuclear testing put dangerous amounts of radioactive materials, including strontium 90, into the atmosphere. Off the coast of California, oil from offshore wells fouled waters and beaches as, elsewhere, did massive spills from the new supertankers. A growing culture of consumption created mountains of solid waste and rivers of sewage. Poisonous chemicals were carelessly buried or left in leaking steel drums to contaminate underground water supplies; one river burst into flame. The production of hazardous substances made workplaces dangerous, even deadly. The country's crops were drenched in insecticides, herbicides, and fertilizers, its livestock infused with synthetic chemicals and hormones.

Americans grew increasingly uneasy about the squandering of the country's once seemingly limitless resources, about the sullying of the landscape by industrial detritus and consumer trash. There was a growing suspicion that something was amiss in our affluent society, that we were fouling our own nest and poisoning our own wells. Our very affluence prompted many Americans to see environmental degradation as an obstacle to their search for a higher standard of living.[4] A growing body of scientific testimony seemed to verify that something was going very wrong. Neo-Malthusians, including Fairfield Osborn,

Garrett Hardin, and Paul Ehrlich, warned that human numbers and consumption were outstripping what the earth could provide in perpetuity. Aldo Leopold's *Sand County Almanac*, an amalgam of science and ethics that is now one of the sacred texts of American environmentalism, admonished that humans are no more and no less than members of the entire community of life. Leopold called for a new land ethic that "changes the role of *Homo sapiens* from conqueror of the land-community to plain member and citizen of it."[5] Barry Commoner, the biologist, author, and political activist, and others pointed out that our technologies were breaking the chemical and biological cycles that sustain the planet. And in her acclaimed book *Silent Spring*, Rachel Carson presented clear, chilling evidence that the destructive technologies deployed by industrial society threatened all life, including human life.[6]

Public concern about the decline of the environment became a flood that could not be contained. It burst over the dam on April 22, 1970—the first Earth Day. Millions of Americans took to the streets and campuses to demonstrate their deep concern and to demand that environmental problems be addressed. On that day, environmentalism emerged for the first time on the national stage as an unmistakable mass social movement. The inchoate fears, anger, and longing of the public had been vivified into a suddenly potent political and economic force.

The immediate effect of the new tide of public opinion was to prod the federal government into action. President Richard Nixon, no "green" radical but keenly attuned to the political zeitgeist, stated that the 1970s "absolutely must be the years when America pays its debt to the past by reclaiming the purity of its air, its water and our living environment. It is literally now or never."[7] By executive order, Nixon created the Environmental Protection Agency, which became the single most effective federal tool for reducing pollution by corporations and municipalities—and for doing the research and education needed to alert the American people about threats to their land, air, water, and health.

Congress responded with a furious burst of bipartisan legislative activism, producing a spate of environmental statutes, from the National Environmental Policy Act of 1969, the Occupational Safety and Health Act of 1970, the Clean Air Act of 1970, and the Federal Water Pollution Control Act Amendments of 1972 to the Alaska National Interest Lands Conservation Act in 1980 and many more in between. In its totality, the explosion of congressional activism that produced these landmark environmental statutes must be considered one of the great legislative achievements in the nation's history.

State and municipal governments, in part because of new regulatory responsibilities passed on to them by Washington, also responded to the rising environmental impulse, creating their own environmental protection agencies and taking initiatives to address problems such as solid waste, compromised drinking water, and the need to provide open space for their citizens.

The new environmentalism emerged out of the social ferment and activism of the 1960s. It was an era of movements, notably the antiwar, civil rights, and feminist movements. Many of the senior cadre of today's major environmental organizations came from the militant campuses of that period. They believed that social change and political activism were the keys to protecting and restoring the environment. Unlike the older conservation groups, their focus was not on land and wildlife preservation but on pollution and toxic substances in the environment and their effects on human health. Out of this social activism sprang new environmental groups, including the Environmental Defense Fund and the Natural Resources Defense Council, whose chief tools were litigation and, later, lobbying for legislation designed to protect the environment. They took their battles to the courts to try to enforce the new environmental laws and to defend citizens threatened by environmental degradation. Other new groups, including Greenpeace, Environmental Action, and Friends of the Earth, used direct action and public information campaigns to alert

Americans to what was being done to the natural world that sustained them.

A number of the national organizations pooled resources to form the League of Conservation Voters in 1970. The league monitored the environmental records of members of Congress and the executive branch and endorsed environmentally minded candidates on a bipartisan basis. Older conservation groups such as the National Wildlife Federation and the National Audubon Society broadened their agendas to take on the new issues of pollution, sprawl, and landscape degradation. The ranks of the environmentalists were reinforced by activists in the scientific community through the Union of Concerned Scientists and Physicians for Social Responsibility.

This period is often described as the "second wave" of environmentalism. Some commentators have called it the "golden age" of environmentalism in the United States, not only because of its legislative and political gains but also because it was a time when environmental quality also became an issue of democracy. Citizens across the country became aware of what was happening to their physical surroundings. Equally important, they also acquired a faith—not always requited— that in the American democracy, change was possible, that they could act as individuals and communities to obtain relief from the environmental dangers with which they were threatened. A watershed event of grass-roots activism captured national attention in 1978 when citizens of Love Canal, a neighborhood in New York, led by a courageous and crafty young housewife named Lois Gibbs, forced the federal government to pay for their evacuation from their houses, which had been built on the site of a toxic waste dump. The Love Canal victory inspirited communities around the country to address their local environmental concerns and drew many new recruits into the growing army of citizen activists.

The golden age of environmentalism, if such it was, came to an abrupt end in 1980 when Ronald Reagan entered the White House. Reagan was a simple man with a simple idea: government had become an unacceptably heavy burden to market capitalism and to the individual freedom of Americans. His goal was to get government off the backs of the people. In practice, this generally meant easing or removing regulatory requirements, particularly environmental regulatory requirements, on industry. He appointed environmental officials, notably Secretary of the Interior James G. Watt and Environmental Protection Agency administrator Anne (Burford) Gorsuch, who devoted their energies to reducing the ability of their agencies to protect natural resources and public health.

At the same time, corporate America, which had been caught off guard by the militant environmentalism that emerged in the 1960s and 1970s, began to mount an effective resistance. The business community, which had originally viewed anti-pollution efforts as a temporary if annoying fad, began to employ sophisticated skills, similar to those it had developed in its successful counterattack on the trade union movement, to fight environmental regulation and to counter the warnings and accusations leveled against it by the environmentalists.

In large part because the American people, alerted by the environmentalists through the news media, were paying attention to what was happening in Washington, President Reagan and his administration were unable to roll back the gains made over the course of the century. In fact, the membership rolls and treasuries of the environmental groups swelled to unheard-of levels as Americans demonstrated their concern by joining in record numbers. Gorsuch and Watt were forced to resign. And George Bush, Reagan's vice president, pledged to be the "environmental president" during his successful first run for the White House. A decade later, the environmental community was again able to rally enough public support to stalemate a ferocious assault on the environmental laws by right-wing radicals who controlled Congress.

In response to the counterattack against them, a number of environmental organizations, chiefly those operating at the national level, sought to develop new skills and tactics. They developed expertise in economic and political analysis, adopted more aggressive media and public outreach strategies, paid at least lip service to the disproportionate ecological ills heaped on the nation's poor and minorities, and looked for ways to achieve their goals without the assistance of the now less-than-sympathetic Congress and courts. Instead of attacking industry's every wrong environmental turn, some environmentalists sought negotiated settlements to pollution problems. The advocacy of market forces—as opposed to command-and-control regulation—as a tool for protecting the environment was a central feature of the new environmentalism.

These tactics were labeled the "third wave" of environmentalism. The most famous (or notorious, depending on one's perspective) example of this approach was the system of tradable air pollution permits proposed by the Environmental Defense Fund and accepted by President Bush and Congress for inclusion in the Clean Air Act Amendments of 1990. Proponents of the third wave called it a response to end-of-century political and economic realities, but it caused sharp divisions within the movement as critics complained that an excess of pragmatism was compromising essential goals. Although the market tools and accommodation tactics of the third wave may have blunted the counterrevolution, these critics say, they caused forward progress in protecting the environment to slow to a painful crawl.

As the 20th century drew to a close, it was clear that environmentalism had wrought profound changes in American life—to its landscape, its institutions, and its people. Since that first Earth Day, well more than one hundred pieces of major federal legislation affecting the environment had become law. Every state and most major cities had some kind of environmental protection agency. Wary politicians and battle-scarred corporations grudgingly conceded that the environmental movement was here to stay and was a potent force to be reckoned with. And given the enormous growth of population and economic activity, of production, consumption, and the generation of waste and pollution in the post–World War II era, imagine what the physical condition of the country would be had it not been for the environmental revolution. That our air is somewhat clearer and more breathable, that our water is somewhat cleaner and more drinkable in many places, that we are not buried in garbage, that some abandoned toxic waste sites have been cleansed, that some of our wildlands have been preserved from development and some of our threatened wildlife has been protected constitute almost miraculous achievements in the face of the economic juggernaut.

Even more significant, perhaps, is that environmentalism has changed the way most Americans look at the world and the way we live our daily lives. Public opinion polls consistently show that a majority of Americans consider themselves to be environmentalists. Most of us now think of a healthy environment as a basic human right. As Writer Mark Dowie noted, "American environmentalism grew to become many things— world view, life style, science; to a few religion; and, eventually, a complex political movement."[8] Joshua Reichert, director of environmental programs for The Pew Charitable Trusts, probably the biggest single contributor to environmental advocacy causes among foundations, called environmentalism "the most significant social movement in America." Political scientist Michael Kraft found that "the environment had become a core part of mainstream American values. . . . It was as close to a consensual issue as one usually finds in U.S. politics."[9]

In the 20th century, environmentalism provided an intellectual and ethical context that enabled Americans, and people in much of the rest of the world, to see the harm that human activity was inflicting on the natural world—and on their own bodies. It established a legal and institutional infrastructure to help them come to grips with these ills and enlisted an army of activists, governmental and nongovernmental, at the local, national, and international levels, to work on solutions. An esoteric enthusiasm for a small elite at the beginning of the century, environmentalism had been transformed into a planet-wide value by its end.

But as a new century unfolds, the environmental movement faces challenging, often frightening, new issues. Problems such as climate change, acid precipitation, disappearing species, vanishing forests, crashing populations of marine life, spreading deserts, loss of topsoil, inadequate drinking water supplies, and dwindling farmland and other open space are compromising the balance of biological systems on the planet, threatening our quality of life, and narrowing the options for the continuing evolution of life, including human life.

At the same time, environmentalists will have to adapt to a rapidly changing economic, political, and social context. The end of the cold war, reawakened religious and ethnic hatreds, globalization of the economy and unchecked growth and concentration of corporate power, continuing inequity in the distribution of the nation's and the planet's wealth, an expected doubling of the world population, the explosion of new information and communication technologies, and the shifting sands of domestic politics all suggest that the voluntary organizations and governmental agencies charged with safeguarding the environment will be required not only to adjust their agenda but also to rethink the very nature of their mission and the means by which they pursue it.

Given the gravity of the problems, if environmentalists and their cause do not prevail in the next few decades, our habitat, our quality of life, and our democratic institutions could erode to the point that they might take centuries to recover. If the world's climate begins to change rapidly and dramatically, if the landscape continues to acidify, if hazardous, gene-altering synthetic substances continue to enter our flesh, if our per capita supplies of food and freshwater continue to dwindle, if we continue to waste nature's bounty and extirpate our biological resources, if we continue to deploy destructive technologies without recognizing their ultimate effects, then our children and grandchildren will live on a hot, dry, hungry, unhealthy, unlovely, and dangerous planet. The harshness of existence in such a world would very likely lead to the disintegration of communal life and the curtailment of personal freedom and opportunity. Environmentalists in that world would be seeking not to protect and restore nature and safeguard human health but to find ways for our posterity to survive amid the wreckage.

It should not come to that. Environmentalism has the latent strength to put us on a course toward a safe and pleasant ecological future, a better, more rational way of living on earth.

First, however, environmentalists will have to learn how to use that strength more wisely and effectively. They will have to find ways to rekindle the transcendental flame lifted by John Muir but now only a spark in their workaday institutions, to recapture the excitement and exhilaration in their cause that Muir found atop his storm-lashed tree. They will have to again practice conservation of the environment as it was envisioned by Roosevelt and Pinchot: as a core value of progressive politics, as an issue of democracy, as a means of bringing science to bear on the creation of policy, and as a means of achieving economic and social equity for present and future generations.

There will have to be yet another wave of environmentalism, one that is broader, more sophisticated, visionary, and aggressive and massive enough to stand against the tide of human numbers and technology, of ignorance and greed and willfulness, that threatens to propel us into an age of physical, biological, and cultural decline.

NOTES

1. George Perkins Marsh, *Man and Nature*, ed. David Lowenthal (1864; reprint, Cambridge, MA: Harvard University Press, Belknap Press, 1965).

2. For a fuller account of the origins and development of the American environmental movement, see, among other sources, Philip Shabecoff, *A Fierce Green Fire*. New York: Hill & Wang, 1993.

3. Robert Gottlieb, *Forcing the Spring: The Transformation of the American Environmental Movement*. Washington, D.C.: Island Press, 1993, pp. 10–11 ff. Gottlieb maintains that these efforts were, in fact, central to environmentalism.

4. Samuel B. Hays, *Beauty, Health, and Permanence*. Cambridge, England: Cambridge University Press, 1987, p. 4.

5. Aldo Leopold, *A Sand County Almanac*. New York: Oxford University Press, 1948, p. 215.

6. Rachel Carson, *Silent Spring,* 25th anniversary ed. Boston: Houghton Mifflin Company, 1987.

7. Quoted in *Congressional Quarterly,* October 30, 1970, p. 2728.

8. Mark Dowie, *Losing Ground.* Cambridge, MA: MIT Press, 1995, p. 27.

9. Michael E. Kraft, *Environmental Policy and Politics.* New York: HarperCollins, 1996, p. 74.

How Does Growing Organic Coffee and Chocolate Help Birds?

How are chocolate and coffee and the birds in your backyard connected? Coffee and cacao trees (which produce chocolate) are grown in tropical areas. Many of the birds we see in the summer spend their winters in these same tropical forests. These tropical forests are some of the most biologically diverse spots on the planet. So what is the problem? Every year, vast areas of rain forest are cleared to plant coffee or cacao trees that then need pesticides and fertilizers to grow and produce our coffee and chocolate. According to the World Watch Institute, almost all of the land used for coffee production is located in current or former rain forest areas.[1] Clearing the rain forests kills many species of plants and animals, and it destroys the habitats for birds that migrate. It also leaves the land more vulnerable to erosion and the coffee and cacao trees themselves more susceptible to disease and drought.

One program designed to protect the rain forests involves the production of shade-grown coffee. In this method, coffee trees are grown and cultivated beneath the shady trees of the native rain forest, rather than in fields that have been cut and cleared specifically to grow coffee plants. Shade-grown coffee is not a new idea, as journalist Paul Tolme explains in the following article. It also has many environmental benefits. Shade-coffee farms harbor more birds than any other agricultural lands. According to studies in Colombia and Mexico, sun-grown coffee plantations support about 95% fewer bird species than shade-grown coffee plantations do.

There are similar programs in place for producing chocolate.[2] The programs serve as an example of how solving one environmental problem can bring about additional environmental and economic benefits.

—The Editor

1. Halweil, Brian. "Why Your Daily Fix Can Fix More Than Your Head." *World Watch Institute Magazine*. May 2002.

2. Bright, Chris. "Chocolate Could Bring the Forest Back." *World Watch Institute Magazine*. December 2001.

3 Gadsby, Patricia. "Endangered Chocolate." *Discover*, Vol. 23. No. 8. August 2002.

Made in the Shade
by Paul Tolme

Every day Americans drink 300 million cups of coffee. Few of them realize their morning ritual could be contributing to the demise of the birds in their own backyards. By making a point of buying only coffee grown under a canopy of trees, they would be helping to save crucial habitat for these migratory species in their winter homes.

The peaks of Mexico's Sierra Madre range rise into the blue haze of a humid Chiapas morning. Beneath them, Bernardo Peters steers his four-wheel-drive vehicle up a rutted mountain road. He stops at a white metal sign, which is neatly hand-lettered *area natural protegida*—"Protected Natural Area"—and turns off the engine, putting hand to ear. "Listen," he says, "to all the birds." As we sit, the distant warbles grow steadily louder, surrounding us like conversations in a crowded restaurant. The birdsong is a fitting welcome to Finca Irlanda, the thriving habitat that is his family's shade-grown-coffee farm.

Walter Peters, Bernardo's 72-year-old father, waits with his trusty German shepherd, Wolf, outside the rambling colonial home that his own father built. Walter is a coffee farmer by trade but a birder at heart, and he wastes no time beginning a tour of the *finca,* or farm. The 720-acre property, where six-foot-high coffee plants and lofty shade trees intermingle, stretches over three sides of a 3,500-foot mountain ridge enclosed in thick rainforest canopy. This is the Soconusco region of the state of Chiapas, which lies in southernmost Mexico. Chiapas not only contains the country's most productive coffee farms—including this one, the main source of Audubon's new organic, shade-grown blend—it is home to eight Important Bird Areas, or land formally identified as critical bird habitat. Sometimes it's difficult to distinguish between the two.

Walter scurries down a terraced slope and raises his binoculars. "Aha," he says, motioning at a flash of yellow feathers. "A western tanager." Seconds later he pivots and points out a wood wren sitting comfortably in an acacia tree. Birding with Walter, whose trim physique and surefootedness testify to a lifetime of climbing these mountains, is an aerobic activity. He stops just long enough to identify nearby birds, then hikes off again, reciting the names of plants and insects along the way.

A broad-winged hawk circles high above a valley. Close by, an American redstart lands in a 100-foot-tall wild avocado tree. A blue-crowned motmot hops along a balsa branch, and the red crest of a lineated woodpecker flickers like flame. Walter shushes his companions and mimics the call of a male trogon, but the yellow-billed, red-bellied beauty refuses his invitation. "Look there," he says, indicating a tree swallow. "They are migrating back to the North." Everywhere we turn we see birds of all colors, sizes, and songs.

The reason is simple. Here, among the branches of a shade-grown-coffee farm and scattered in the leaf litter that covers its soil, is a smorgasbord of insects, nectar, and fruit. This is not undisturbed forest. This is human-managed habitat—an agricultural endeavor—but it's valuable to wildlife all the same. As deforestation continues apace elsewhere in Latin America, this ecosystem exists because a farmer cared to create it, and because people throughout the United States choose to drink his coffee.

Shade-coffee farms shelter more birds than any other agricultural landscape; only untamed tropical forests have greater diversity.

WALTER PETERS ISN'T REVOLUTIONIZING THE WAY COFFEE IS GROWN

Until about 30 years ago farmers worldwide cultivated *Coffea arabica*—a wild forest shrub from the highlands of Ethiopia—under a shade canopy. Leafy tropical trees play an important role in protecting the health of the farm. At Finca Irlanda, 70 species—natives like Mexican cedar and inga, and fruit trees like mango—shelter coffee plants from sun and rain, stabilize soil on erosion-prone slopes, and snuff the growth of weeds. Their falling leaves return nutrients to the soil.

Just as a building with many floors and types of apartments houses more people, a forest with trees of varying heights and species provides habitat for more animals. The complexity of the best shade-coffee farms extends right down to more than 100 species of plants, from camedor palms and wild orchids to flowering philodendrons that cling to the trunks of trees. At Finca Irlanda, a recent study of the insects and spiders taking advantage of this diversity revealed 793 species. Animals such as the ocelot and the endangered *Tamandua mexicana*—a tree-climbing anteater—have been found on shade-coffee farms, too.

An important choice is brewing: Continue to drink coffee without considering how it is grown, or deliberately seek out brands that are grown in ways that protect migratory birds.

But as I trek across the ridge with Walter, the alarm calls and indignant flutters of the *finca*'s avian inhabitants grab my attention most. Shade-coffee farms shelter more birds than any other agricultural landscape; only untamed tropical forests have greater diversity. As these forests are cleared for grazing, agriculture, timber, and development, shade-coffee farms demonstrate how a farmer can work the land while also protecting biodiversity.

Walter has counted more than 200 species of birds during his lifetime here. Most are residents such as yellow-naped parrots, orange-chinned parakeets, and long-tailed manakins, but there are also 60 species of neotropical migrants. It is these birds that connect Finca Irlanda to backyards across the United States. Some migratory species, like the ovenbird and the wood thrush, are feeling the pressure of habitat fragmentation on both their breeding and wintering grounds. For these birds, shade-grown-coffee farms can serve as a crucial refuge.

The problem is that not all coffee is grown this way. On plantations in Brazil and Vietnam, two of the world's leading producers, rows of coffee stretch on for miles, like corn in Iowa. The land has been cleared of trees and planted in giant monocultures, exposed to full sun. This practice, called "technified" or "intensive" production, requires new sun-tolerant varieties of coffee coupled with the routine use of chemical fertilizers and pesticides (in part to replace the natural mulching and pest control provided by the trees). Of the permanent cropland planted in coffee, 17 percent in Mexico, 40 percent in Costa Rica, and 69 percent in Colombia is now grown in full sun.

These plantations accomplished what the coffee growers had set out to do—produce bigger and bigger yields. Today, with a double latte for sale on almost every corner, coffee is one of the world's most valuable legally traded commodities. But this development came at a cost. The soil on these coffee plantations is less productive and more easily eroded; the coffee plants are less resilient during the dry season and must be replaced more often. And according to studies in Colombia and Mexico, these plantations support 94 percent to 97 percent fewer bird species than shade-coffee farms. "It's a sonic desert," says ornithologist Thomas Dietsch, a postdoctoral fellow with the Smithsonian Migratory Bird Center who did avian surveys on both sun and shade-grown farms. "Every once in a while a bird will pop up from the coffee understory, but seeing birds within your 25-meter radius is not very common."

Coffee farms have replaced mountain forests across much of the Coffee Belt, between the tropics of Cancer and Capricorn, where growing conditions are ideal and frosts are rare. More than 25 million people rely on coffee farming for their income, and about 30 million acres worldwide are devoted to the crop.

"Making coffee farmers allies in conserving wildlife habitat is without question one of the most important challenges in tropical conservation," says Chris Wille, chief of sustainable agriculture for the Rainforest Alliance, "and one that has out-standing potential for landscape-wide benefits."

"We don't just sell coffee. We sell the opportunity for the consumer to buy a concept: a fair, organic, bird-friendly, and sustainable product. That is what we sell in every cup."

For Americans, who consume a third of the world's coffee—300 million cups a day—an important choice is brewing: Continue to drink coffee without considering how it is grown, or deliberately seek out brands that are grown in ways that protect migratory birds and other species. Luckily, you can have your espresso and drink it, too, because of certification programs run by two respected conservation organizations.

The Smithsonian Migratory Bird Center launched its Bird Friendly program in the mid-1990s, and the Rainforest Alliance soon followed suit with a certification program of its own. Both groups send auditors to farms to ensure they maintain a multitiered forest canopy, which is where two-thirds of the birds on any shade-coffee farm live. Consumers need to look for the Bird Friendly or Rainforest Alliance seals on the package to be certain the coffee inside measures up. "You can go into any supermarket and find coffee labeled as shade-grown," Dietsch says. But without a certification stamp, "the words mean nothing."

There is a difference behind the seals. The Smithsonian standards also require farms to be organic (although other certified-organic coffees aren't necessarily shade-grown). This primarily means that growers cannot apply chemical pesticides or fertilizers, which kill insects beneficial to birds and may run off to contaminate watersheds. While the Rainforest Alliance does not require its farms to meet strict organic standards, it sets guidelines for conserving soil and wildlife, and insists that farm managers use the safest agrochemicals according to strictly monitored guidelines. In addition, the Rainforest Alliance program covers social and labor issues—such as ensuring fair wages and safe working conditions, and providing workers with health care and better housing. Finca Irlanda is certified by both groups.

For now, shade-grown coffee is still a niche market. Roughly 19 million pounds of Rainforest Alliance–certified coffee, and an additional 3.75 million pounds that is certified Bird Friendly, were shipped this past year. Those are collectively but a drip in the carafe of global production—roughly 13 billion pounds a year. One explanation is that conservation-minded coffee drinkers "haven't yet flexed their muscles," says Wille. "If they do, their potential to change the coffee business is tremendous."

To be sure, the 71 million Americans who consider themselves birdwatchers represent a huge, untapped market.

To some extent, the industry is waking up to smell the coffee before their customers are. "Every coffee company has sustainability on its radar now, and nearly all of them are trying to do something," says Wille. "The boldest are going for certification. The boldest of all—Kraft—has jumped into sustainable sourcing and equity along the supply chain with both feet."

One of the largest coffee roasters in the world, Kraft Foods has committed to buying 15 million pounds of Rainforest Alliance–certified coffee over the next three years. The company will launch a shade-grown brand in Europe this fall, and in the United States it already has a certified product available to institutional buyers such as schools. Perhaps more important, some of these beans will be mixed into mainstream blends like Maxwell House, indicating a change in how Kraft sources all of its coffee—not just specialty brands. Another global roaster, Procter & Gamble, has also been testing the shade-grown waters. A Rainforest Alliance–certified Signature Roast of its Millstone brand will soon be available in stores (it's already available online).

Consumers used to buying $3 tins of supermarket coffee, however, should be prepared to pay more for coffee that's shade-grown and organic; these beans are more expensive because they cost twice as much to grow. Finca Irlanda, for instance, requires about 300 days of labor per acre compared with about 150 on neighboring conventional farms. Instead of applying herbicides, workers cut weeds from between coffee plants with machetes. It costs Finca Irlanda about $1.39 to produce a pound of coffee, compared with 60 cents or less on mechanized sun farms.

Finca Irlanda stays in business because it receives $1.90 per pound from its American roaster, the Rogers Family Coffee Companies of San Francisco. The Rogers Charitable Fund, the family's foundation, spends an additional 20 cents per pound enhancing life in Finca Irlanda's coffee-farm community. This year the money will cover the costs of a preschool nursery with a kitchen that will provide breakfast and lunch for the nursery and the entire elementary school.

Many farms don't have the advantage of such altruistic middlemen. A worldwide glut of cheaply produced beans has depressed prices to record lows, prompting industry watchers to declare a coffee crisis. The World Bank estimates that 600,000 Central American workers have lost jobs as small coffee farms have gone bankrupt or switched to cattle, corn, or even coca. Displaced workers often flee to the United States.

Guaranteeing farmers a minimum price, and a livable income, is at the heart of a movement known as "fair trade"— another label that can be found on coffees, alone or along with shade-grown or organic certifications. TransFair, the leading fair trade certifier, requires that buyers pay a just amount for a given product, helping small-scale, traditional growers survive in a world of increasing scale and mechanization. For coffee, this amounts to at least $1.26 per pound, which is divided between individual farmers and the cooperatives they belong to.

Fair trade is one arena in which coffeehouses have begun to exercise their sizeable influence. Dunkin' Donuts, the number one retailer of coffee-by-the-cup in America, buys only TransFair–certified beans for the espresso-based drinks it is rolling out in 4,000 stores across the country. The chain anticipates selling 30 million fair trade lattes and cappuccinos this year alone. Starbucks, the world's leading retailer of specialty coffee, doubled the amount of fair trade-certified coffee it buys, from roughly 1 million pounds in 2002 to 2.1 million pounds in 2003. Last year it also purchased more than 1.8 million pounds of beans grown by small-scale farmers in the buffer zone of El Triunfo Biosphere Reserve in Chiapas—a flagship project of Conservation International's Conservation Coffee program, which promotes coffee grown under the protection of shade.

This is a heartening trend for farmers like Bernardo Peters. "If I get good prices and good contracts," he explains, "I can improve the environment, protect the birds, improve the lives of my workers. If I don't get good contracts, I can do none of this, and all the young men leave for the North."

Walter's father, German immigrant Rodolfo Peters, could scarcely have predicted how intense the world's coffee addiction would become when he first bought the *finca* from an Irishman (thus *Irlanda*) in 1929. Walter took over the family farm in the 1960s and, aside from five years in Mexico City for schooling and then two years in Germany to learn his family's native tongue, he has spent his entire life studying birds among the coffee.

Thirty families live and work on the farm year-round, but the workforce swells to 500 during the fall harvest. Workers pick the fleshy red fruits, called cherries, and place them in large fermenting tanks, where the pulpy layer around the beans softens. The cherries are then raked onto a concrete patio and left in the sun. A rotating drum removes the parchmentlike layer from the dried beans, which are sorted by hand for quality. The beans are then poured into burlap bags for export to Europe, the United States, or Japan.

Finca Irlanda shipped the world's first batch of certified-organic coffee beans, in 1967, when other farms were beginning to descend the slippery agricultural slope of dousing their fields with chemicals. Walter runs his hands through the rich black compost that makes organic farming possible on his finca. Since the bean makes up just one-third of the cherry's weight, gargantuan piles of pulp are left over. These are mixed with weeds and with the manure from the 40 head of cattle that supply meat for the farm. The resulting natural fertilizer is used to grow seedlings of both native trees and coffee.

For all his efforts, Walter is frustrated that so many bird species are not as pervasive as they once were. There are fewer black-throated green warblers and Tennessee warblers every year, and Walter saw only one American kestrel last winter. As a young man he used to see scarlet macaws all the time; now he's lucky to see any at all. He mimics the descent of a diving bird with his hand. "The trend," he says, "is always down."

Surely blame lies with deforestation and development. But, he'll remind you, full-sun plantations on the birds' wintering grounds have taken a toll as well. Back at the house, father and son discuss the challenge of educating consumers. On a small scale, ecotourism may offer one answer. The family is readying several rooms for tourists curious about the workings, and wildlife, of an organic, shade-grown-coffee farm. Other *fincas* in the region also hope that "agricultural tourism" will help pay for costly certification.

After all, connoisseurs do value the label. Specialty coffees—shade-grown, organic, and fair trade—taste better, they swear. Under the cover of trees, coffee cherries are allowed to ripen slowly; only the most mature ones are picked. And like wine and honey, these small-batch coffees have a distinctive taste associated with the microclimates in which they are grown. But good beans are only part of the equation. "We don't just sell coffee," Bernardo says, hoisting a cup. "We sell the opportunity for the consumer to buy a concept: a fair, organic, bird-friendly, and sustainable product. That is what we sell in every cup." He takes a sip and smiles. "And it's delicious."

Leaving Finca Irlanda, I vow to never again buy cheap, sun-grown coffee. Without consumer support, small farms that protect biodiversity can't compete with technified plantations whose main objective is profit. By choosing beans grown in a manner that steps lightly on the land, Americans can help ensure that the backyard birds they watch while sipping their morning brew will still be there for future generations. Certified shade-grown coffee is more than delicious. It is strong.

Section B

The Oceans

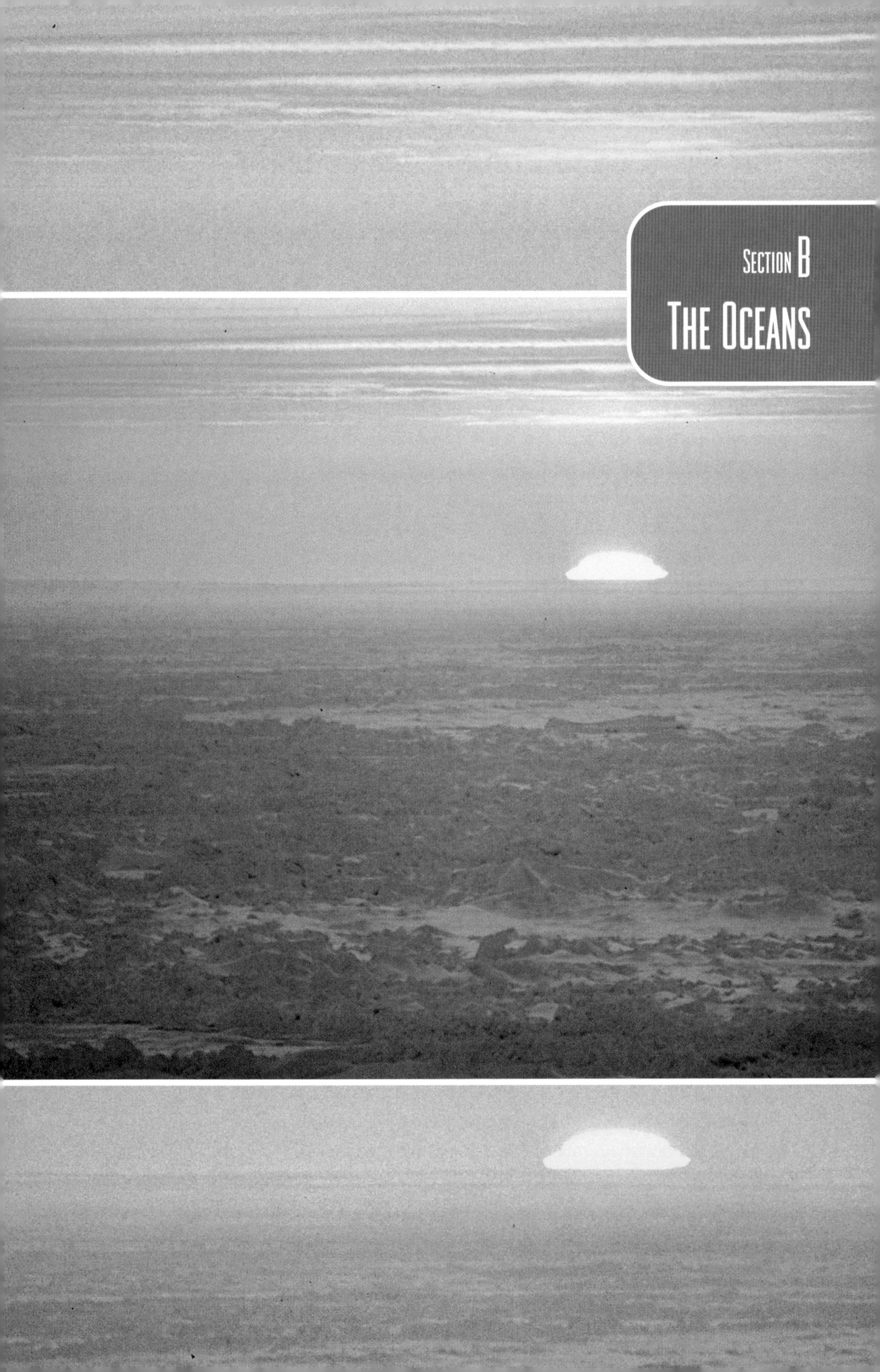

Do We Need to Protect Our Oceans?

In 1949, scientist and conservationist Aldo Leopold introduced Americans to the need to develop a land ethic. By this, he meant that people who take things from the Earth have a responsibility to consider the effect their actions have on the land.[1] In 1983, Americans followed Leopold's advice and took responsibility for an area of the Earth that is larger than the land area of the United States. President Ronald Reagan declared the entire ocean area that stretches for 200 nautical miles around U.S. borders as an Exclusive Economic Zone (EEZ)—meaning that only Americans could use its resources. How are we doing with this huge responsibility for underwater land?

In June 2000, 18 members of the Pew Oceans Commission began the first review of U.S. ocean policy in over 30 years. (The Pew Oceans Commission is an independent environmental group devoted to protecting living sea resources.) The members of the commission came from all areas: fishing, science, conservation, government, education, and business. They traveled the country, talking to anyone they could find with connections to the oceans, from fishermen to farmers.

The oceans are huge, and so are their problems. The commission's 2003 report, *America's Living Ocean: Charting a Course for Sea Change*, identified several areas of concern, which will be seen in the following excerpt. Nonpoint source pollution, or the oils and fertilizers that just run off the land into the water, causes much damage. Point source pollution, like animal feedlots and ships, is another threat to water quality. Introduced species, or plants and animals that come originally from other places, crowd out or kill the native plants and animals that already live in a place. In addition, climate change is causing a rise in ocean temperatures. This will not only raise the sea level but will dramatically change fisheries and the way nutrients are cycled in the water. Other issues outlined in the report are habitat alteration, overfishing and by-catch (when other species are killed in the process of fishing), and coastal development.

It will take a serious commitment by communities, nations, and independent organizations to protect the vast resource the oceans represent. But along with the many problems the commission identified, its members found "a shared sense of urgency and commitment to reverse the decline in the health of the oceans."

—The Editor

1. Leopold, Aldo. *A Sand County Almanac*. New York: Oxford University Press,1949.

American's Living Oceans: Charting a Course for Sea Change
from the Pew Oceans Commission

The oceans are our largest public domain. America's oceans span nearly 4.5 million square miles, an area 23 percent larger than the nation's land area. Their biological riches surpass those of our national forests and wilderness areas. The genetic, species, habitat, and ecosystem diversity of the oceans is believed to exceed that of any other Earth system. Yet, incredibly, we are squandering this bounty. Humanity's numbers and the technological capacity of our age result in unprecedented impact upon the oceans and coasts. The disturbing signs of these impacts can be found nearly everywhere we look.

Most obviously we are depleting the oceans of fish, and have been for decades. The government can only assure us that 22 percent of managed fish stocks are being fished sustainably.

The decline of New England fisheries is most notorious. By 1989, New England cod, haddock, and yellowtail flounder had reached historic lows.

In U.S. waters, Atlantic halibut are commercially extinct—too rare to justify a directed fishing effort. In addition, by the mid-1990s, we halved the breeding population of Atlantic swordfish. However, such problems are by no means limited to the East Coast. In September 2002, the government imposed substantial restrictions on bottom fishing along the West Coast in an attempt to save four of the most depleted rockfish species. Populations of bocaccio rockfish, commonly sold as Pacific red snapper, have been driven to less than 10 percent of their historic numbers.

One can find stories about the effects of development, pollution, and overfishing all along our coastal waters—from Alaska to the Gulf of Mexico to Hawaii's coral reefs. Often the tale begins far inland.

The greatest pollution threat to coastal marine life today is the runoff of excess nitrogen from fertilized farm fields, animal feedlots, and urban areas. Airborne nitrogen—from industrial smokestacks, automobile exhaust pipes, and ammonia rising from huge manure lagoons—is also deposited in the ocean. Just as they fertilize the land, nutrients fertilize coastal waters, and excess amounts can cause massive blooms of algae. These blooms can trigger a chain of events that deplete the ocean waters of oxygen, turning vast areas into hypoxic areas, also known as dead zones. Some of these algal blooms produce toxins that can be fatal to fish, marine mammals, and occasionally people.

The deaths of one million menhaden in North Carolina's Pamlico Sound in 1991, 150 endangered Florida manatees in 1996, and 400 California sea lions along the central California coast in 1998 have all been attributed to harmful algal blooms. They disrupt aquaculture, wild fisheries, and coastal tourism. In the past two decades, their effects have expanded from a few scattered coastal areas to nearly all coastal states. But they are only one of the many human-related impacts that are transforming our coasts.

Coastal counties are now home to more than half of the U.S. population. Another 25 million people will live along the coast by 2015, further straining our wetlands, mangrove forests, estuaries, coral reefs, and other coastal habitats.

Florida has experienced some of the nation's most rapid coastal development. From 1940 to 1996, the state population increased 700 percent, from 1.8 million to 14.3 million. Development has altered both water quality and water quantity, leading to the loss of more than half of the Everglades, the largest contiguous wetland in the U.S. Freshwater flow through the Everglades has declined by approximately 70 percent since the 1940s and the population of wading birds has dropped by 90 percent.

Much of Florida's development has been concentrated in 16 southern counties that extend from Lake Okeechobee to the Florida Keys. The marine ecosystems of the Keys are now undergoing rapid and profound changes.

Scientists recently conducted extensive surveys at 160 monitoring stations throughout the Florida Keys. They found that both the number of diseased areas of coral and of the number of diseased coral species had increased dramatically from 1996 to 1998. About 75 percent of the coral species in the Florida Keys show symptoms of a variety of diseases. In addition, two-thirds of the monitoring stations lost species between 1996 and 2000, and the total stony coral cover had decreased by about 40 percent between 1996 and 1999. Scientists do not know why so many species have simultaneously become susceptible to disease.

Our current state of knowledge makes it difficult to unravel the relative roles of natural processes and human influence, whether from chemical pollution, nutrient enrichment, or climate change. But scientists are finding increasing human influence on the environment.

For example, in Puget Sound, PCB [polychlorinated biphenyl] contamination may be a factor in the decline of orcas, or killer whales, whose numbers have declined by 14 percent since 1995. PCB levels in the Puget Sound population exceed that known to suppress immune function in another marine mammal, the harbor sea. Similarly, increased levels of PCBs, DDT [a pesticide, now banned in the United States], and tributyltin (a component in boat paint) may be contributing to the deaths of California southern sea otters. Scientists have also discovered that increasing sea-surface temperatures are associated with the northern spread of a pathogen that attacks the eastern oyster. The pathogen, *Perkinsus marinus*, was itself likely introduced into the U.S. Atlantic and Gulf coasts via aquaculture.

The crisis in our oceans is such that many marine populations and ecosystems may be reaching the point where even a small disturbance can cause a big change. We must therefore initiate large changes ourselves, not in the oceans, but in our governance of them and our attitude toward them. We must no longer structure our thinking in terms of maximizing the short-term commercial benefit we derive from the oceans, but rather in terms of maximizing the health and persistence of ocean ecosystems.

Addressing the crisis of our seas will require a serious rethinking of ocean law, informed by a new ocean ethic. The legal framework that governs our oceans is more than 30 years old, and has not been updated to reflect the current state of ocean resources or our values toward them. The last comprehensive review of our ocean policy was completed in 1969, when the Stratton Commission produced its seminal report, *Our Nation and the Sea.* The recommendations of the Stratton Commission, including the establishment of the National Oceanic and Atmospheric Administration [NOAA] and the enactment of the Coastal Zone Management Act, provided the blueprint for U.S. ocean policy. But our oceans and coasts—and our society as well—have changed dramatically since that time. For example, nearly 30 years ago, in response to outrage over foreign overfishing of abundant fish populations off America's shores, Congress took action to develop a domestic fishing industry and capture the wealth of fisheries for this country. Today, the problem is reversed. We are overfishing our already depleted fish populations, harming marine ecosystems, and leaving fishermen out of work.

Over the past three decades our understanding of the oceans has also evolved. For too long we viewed the ocean as a limitless resource. We now know that ocean life is finite. We overlooked the connections between the land and sea. Now, we know that our activities on land—from building roads to logging trees to damming rivers—have a direct impact on the oceans.

Over time, experience on land has made biologists and ecologists aware of the many linkages within and among ecosystems, fostering development of a more sophisticated approach called ecosystem-based management.

An ecosystem is composed of all of the organisms living in a certain place and their interactions with each other and with their environment. Weather, currents, seafloor topography, and human activities are all important influences on ecosystems. The goal of ecosystem-based management is to maintain the health of the whole as well as the parts. It acknowledges the connections among things.

Maintaining healthy ecosystems is crucial. When we sacrifice healthy ecosystems, we must also be prepared to sacrifice economic and social stability. Indeed, once an ecosystem collapses, it may take decades or centuries for it to recover, and the species that we so valued may be permanently lost. The story of horseshoe crabs is a cautionary tale. Every spring, hundreds of thousands of horseshoe crabs migrate to the shores of the Delaware Bay to spawn. The crabs pile up on the beaches, where each female may lay up to 80,000 eggs. When they spawn, as many as 1.5 million migrating shorebirds stop on the beaches to gorge themselves on the eggs. Some species, such as red knots, nearly double their weight during a two-week stopover on their migration from southern Brazil to Canada. If the birds are unable to bulk up on the eggs, they may never complete their flight north, or may fail to breed once they arrive. Small mammals, diamondback terrapins, and mollusks also feed on the eggs.

By the mid-1990s, scientists began to notice declines in horseshoe crab and shorebird counts. The declines coincided with an increase in offshore trawling for the crabs, which are sold as bait to catch eels and whelks. According to the National Marine Fisheries Service, the catch of horseshoe crabs in New Jersey, Delaware, and Maryland doubled between 1990 and 1994 to at least a half million crabs a year. During this period, horseshoe crab counts on spawning beaches were down dramatically, on some beaches by 90 percent. The number of shorebirds declined sharply as well. Also threatened is a multimillion-dollar ecotourism industry centered on the annual bird migrations.

TOWARD AN OCEAN ETHIC

In July 2000, the Pew Oceans Commission embarked on a journey of inquiry. We sought to understand the state of our oceans and the effectiveness of the nation's ocean policy. Our approach encompassed extensive research, consultation with scientific and policy experts, and testimony from Americans whose lives are intertwined with the ocean. We identified three primary problems with ocean governance. The first is its focus on exploitation of ocean resources with too little regard for environmental consequences. The second is its fragmented nature—institutionally, legislatively, and geographically. Third is its focus on individual species as opposed to the larger ecosystems that produce and nurture all life in the sea.

To correct this situation, we have identified five main challenges and corresponding recommendations for revising our laws and institutions. The five challenges are: reforming ocean governance, restoring America's fisheries, protecting our coasts, cleaning coastal waters, and guiding sustainable aquaculture.

New laws and policies, however substantial, are not enough. A more fundamental change is needed. A change in values—not only what we value, but how we value—is essential to protecting and restoring our oceans and coasts.

Our society needs an ethic of stewardship and responsibility toward the ocean and its inhabitants. Like the conservation land ethic that has taken shape in our nation over many decades, an ocean ethic provides a moral framework to guide the conduct of individuals and society. Extending environmental protection beyond a single medium—such as air, or water, or a single species of plant or animal—to entire ecosystems is both a practical measure and our moral obligation as the stewards of our planet.

Why Are Coral Reefs So Important to People and to the Environment?

People can easily see when an entire forest is cut down, or when a field of soil blows away, or a river catches on fire from pollution. Although they are tucked under the ocean and hidden from plain view, coral reefs are in no less danger than these other natural resources. Rod Salm, a marine ecologist with The Nature Conservancy, explains that corals have been subjected to over-fishing, poisoning, dynamiting, and siltation from eroded lands. As explained in the following article, "Rescuing Reefs in Hot Water," his mission is to help save coral reefs.

Coral reefs are huge areas created as living corals secrete calcium carbonate. They form some of the oldest and most diverse ecosystems on Earth. Coral reefs attract such diversity of life that they have been called the "rain forests of the ocean." As in rain forests, there are thought to be millions of species living in coral reefs that have not yet been identified. And, like the rain forests, coral reefs are an important source of medicines. Coral reefs also help protect the coasts from erosion. In addition, healthy reefs provide a huge tourist industry, worth billions of dollars a year in the Florida Keys alone.[1] The reef resources in the United States and its territories contribute an estimated $375 billion to the U.S. economy every year.[2] Despite all the benefits they provide, the reef ecosystems are under threat.

Rod Salm has studied the problems of coral bleaching, which occurs when the zooxanthellae, plant-like organisms that grow in the coral, die. When this happens, the corals lose their photo-synthetic energy source and become vulnerable to damage from sunlight and pollution. But Salm's scientific observations give him reason for hope. Trying to determine what makes reefs resistant to bleaching and what allows them to recover helps scientists to choose areas to protect as marine sanctuaries. As Salm says, using solid science improves the prospects for the long-term survival of coral reefs.

Some formal steps toward protecting reefs started in 1972, when Congress passed the National Marine Sanctuaries Act to help manage designated areas. Today, the United States has 13 marine sanctuaries, taking up a total area about the size of the states of New Hampshire and Vermont combined.[3] In 1998, the U.S. Coral Reef Task Force (USCRTF) was formed to study the issues surrounding endangered reefs and to find ways to protect them. In 2004, Rod Salm announced a partnership between The Nature Conservancy and Conservation International called Transforming Coral Reefs Conservation (TCRC).[4] Currently, less than 1% of the world's oceans is part of Marine Protected Areas. Environmental scientists hope this number will grow as organizations, communities, and governments come together to support a global initiative to create 50 Marine Protected Areas. These sites will serve as a base from which more protected areas can be designated.

—The Editor

1. National Oceanic and Atmospheric Administration (NOAA). Coral Reef Conservation Program Factsheets. Available online at *http://www.coralreef.noaa.gov/*.

2. National Oceanic and Atmospheric Administration (NOAA). Marine Sanctuaries Factsheets. Available online at *http://www.sanctuaries.nos.noaa.gov/*.

3. Agary, Tundi. "America's Coral Reefs: Awash with Problems." *Issues in Science and Technology*. Winter 2003.

4. "Post Script: Relief for Reefs." *The Nature Conservancy*. 2004. Available online at *http://nature.org/magazine/fall2002/coralreefs/people/index.html*.

Rescuing Reefs in Hot Water
by Soames Summerhays

Fantasy reefscapes of turrets, plates, brains and fans—some the size of boulders, others as delicate as lace—compose the coral kingdom of Palau. Brightly painted butterflyfish of a dozen varieties color the coral gardens. Tiny black humbugs with startling white spots peek through the coral branches.

There are thousands of reasons why the Pacific archipelago of Palau, in Micronesia, has been deemed one of the seven Underwater Wonders of the World. Here, in this locus of biodiversity, biologists have so far tallied 385 species of stony coral, 1,387 species of fish and countless other life forms.

Yet there are nearly as many good reasons why Palau is also now a focus of anxiety amid a worldwide epidemic of coral reef decay. Among Palau's vibrant reefs are scenes of devastation. Thickets of corals lie as jumbled rubble, their skeletons veiled by a film of algae and silt sprouting with seaweed. Decimated of diversity, these reefs harbor a wrasse here, a blenny there and a few damselfish picking away at the ruins.

"You'll still see some of the world's most stunning coral reefs in Palau," declares Rod Salm, a marine ecologist with The Nature Conservancy, "but you'll also witness the devastating effects of coral bleaching."

For the past two decades, Salm and his colleagues have watched helplessly as one coral reef after another has been bleached and destroyed by unusually high water temperatures, often associated with the anomalous mix of weather and currents called El Niño. Along with the infamous El Niño of 1998 came the worst worldwide bleaching episode on record, when 85 percent of the corals on many reefs in the Indian Ocean died, coinciding with other crashes across the Pacific and the Caribbean. In a matter of a few months, reefs lost much of their living corals.

With forecasts of a changing climate—and, with it, more frequent El Niños and warmer waters—conservation of coral reefs had suddenly become a demoralizing riddle: how on Earth to save the world's reefs from something as omnipresent as ocean currents. As bleak as the task seemed in the wake of 1998's die-off, one man who was closely watching the destruction may have uncovered a reason for hope in a theory so simple it was nearly overlooked.

PARADISE FADING

Salm grew up fishing and snorkeling along the bountiful Mozambique coastline, an experience that fired his early passion for marine conservation. Graduating from the University of Natal in South Africa with a bachelor's degree in marine biology, he set sail on the *Lindblad Explorer*, a ship pioneering ecotourism expeditions that visited remote and pristine coral reefs around the world. Following his doctorate, Salm went to work for the International Union for the Conservation of Nature and the World Wildlife Fund, locating and designing marine protected areas among exotic archipelagos in the Indian Ocean from eastern Africa to Indonesia.

"I have always been interested in the big picture about how coral reefs function and what causes them to malfunction," says Salm. "I remember, on one of my first assignments, I witnessed how goats destroyed a Mozambique reef by eating the vegetation that, in turn, led to erosion, siltation and the destruction of the corals. It was specifically this kind of observation and analysis that opened my eyes to what was happening during coral bleaching. Mind you, it took time to make sense of it all."

Salm first witnessed coral bleaching in 1990, at the mouth of the Arabian Gulf in Oman. In the years that followed, the bleaching events became more frequent and more destructive. It was well known that the effects of bleaching were patchy, so the attention of the scientific community focused on the areas and species that were hardest hit.

"My colleagues and I had been watching this devastation of coral reefs worldwide with mounting alarm," says Salm, "and for years we had no solution. There has been nothing more frustrating and dismaying than to be faced with a problem that, despite our best efforts, was turning up every few years and capriciously destroying years of conservation work. But could we predict where coral bleaching would occur and where it wouldn't? This was the question I kept asking myself."

A FRAGILE ALLIANCE

Given the corals' ancient lineage and the ecological stability needed to foster such unparalleled diversity, their sudden demise was all the more mysterious and unsettling. They had been forming reefs and surviving calamities for more than 200 million years. Circling the globe in warm shallow waters of the tropics, they provide food and shelter for a stunning array of life. In an acre or two of coral reef in Southeast Asia, for example, there may be as many varieties of fish as there are species of birds in North America. Some scientists estimate that 1 million to 3 million marine species live among the reefs—more species, perhaps, than live in tropical rain forests.

The secret of corals' evolutionary success lies in the mutually beneficial relationship between coral polyps—the individual coral animals—and their one-celled partners, zooxanthellae pronounced zo-zan-THEL-lee). Living within the coral's tissue, the colorful, plantlike zooxanthellae exchange food for shelter, processing sunlight to manufacture 95 percent of the energy the corals need to survive and build their white limestone skeletons.

Corals eventually die without their resident zooxanthellae, which are expelled when water temperatures and light levels increase even slightly. When that happens, corals lose their color as well as their sunscreen, becoming vulnerable to the harmful effects of direct sunlight. Once sea-surface temperatures return to normal, some bleached corals recover their zooxanthellae and their color. Others die.

Many surviving corals will not breed for a year or two after bleaching, reducing a reef's capacity to regenerate. And some scientists predict El Niños will continue to increase in frequency. The Global Coral Reef Monitoring Network predicts that 40 percent of coral reefs will be lost by 2010, "unless urgent management action is taken." Says Steve Coles, a research zoologist at the Bishop Museum in Hawaii who has studied corals' tolerance to temperature, "I think many of us are concerned that if the frequency of El Niños keep increasing, the long-term ability of corals to regenerate may be in question."

Already, bleaching has radically reduced the abundance of some of the most common corals, such as staghorn, and pushed others to the edge of extinction. Peter Glynn of the University of Miami's Rosenstiel School of Marine and Atmospheric Science has documented at least one species of hydrocoral, *Millepora boschmai*, that may have become extinct because of bleaching since the El Niño of 1997–98.

"Anyone diving on a coral reef for the first time today would be blown away by the spectacular life around him," declares Salm. "However, I can assure you from personal experience, in just my lifetime many coral reefs are shadows of their former glory."

"Corals have weathered a catalogue of abuse from overfishing, poisoning, dynamiting, siltation from deforested land and many other people pressures exacting a terrible toll," says Salm. "Now we are faced by this new threat of coral bleaching, which makes other pressures seem trivial by comparison. Furthermore, it is not just bleaching, it is what bleaching precipitates."

Corals that lose their zooxanthellae also lose their resistance to disease. So afterward, even though corals may look robust, they are extremely vulnerable to pollution. Billy Causey, superintendent of the Florida Keys National Marine Sanctuary, has seen an escalation of bleaching since he first recorded it in 1970. He's also seen a rise in the incidence of such lethal diseases as black band and white plague. Since 1996, the sanctuary has lost more than one-third of its living coral cover.

The death of the coral triggers a domino effect among reef organisms. Fish that feed on corals, or take shelter among them, disappear as the corals crumble. With the fate of the reefs go their accompanying tourism and fishing economies. In Australia, the Great Barrier Reef Marine Park Authority estimates that the more than $1 billion in annual revenue derived from reef tourism exceeds that from its fisheries five times over. A World Resources Institute publication, *Reefs at Risk*, estimates that reefs are worth about $375 billion a year worldwide; in developing countries, coral reefs contribute 25 percent of the fish people consume.

A BEACON IN THE RUBBLE

During 1998, at the height of the bleaching episode, Salm was working on an island reef in Kenya. He noted that although the reef facing the open ocean was badly bleached, the reef facing the coast had escaped with only minor damage. But why?

Still looking for answers, Salm joined the Conservancy in the summer of 1999. Dogged by the grim statistics of coral casualties, he made a whirlwind tour of the Conservancy's marine protected areas, first in Indonesia, then the Solomon Islands and, finally, Palau.

In the wreckage that followed bleaching events, Salm discovered a mysterious inconsistency. Diving among the battered reefs of Palau—some of which had lost 99 percent of their corals—Salm learned to look for survivors in unlikely places.

Says Salm, "It really struck home when I visited a forest of monstrous staghorn coral that was totally devastated, on a reef that I would have expected to survive since it had been reserved by the Palauans as a marine park. Yet other reefs, in places far more heavily used, seemed barely affected. Again, I wondered why."

Recalling survey reports from the Indian Ocean, where, on many reefs, 85 percent of the corals had died, Salm had a flash of inspiration. If 85 percent of a reef's corals were destroyed, the upside was that 15 percent had survived. In turning the problem on its head, he found a window of hope for coral reefs. It was on that resistant 15 percent—the survivors that everybody had been ignoring—that the future might be built.

As Salm surveyed other reefs in Palau, he discovered that corals adjacent to cool, upwelling waters appeared to have escaped El Niño unscathed. Upwellings, he inferred, brought relief to the corals. Reefs scoured by strong currents also seemed to have escaped. Could the currents have washed away toxins or stirred cool waters with the warm? Salm found that reefs with cloudy water or where the corals were shaded seemed immune as well. Perhaps turbidity and shade provide a sunscreen, he reasoned, protecting the corals from damaging light.

Salm tested his ideas among the reefs of Indonesia's Komodo National Park. There he found corals surviving under conditions similar to those in Palau. "It was a heady moment," recalls Salm. "On one reef after another, my hypotheses worked."

"I began to check the literature for other scientists' observations, and, while nobody specifically reported where or why corals survived, indirectly, by what they did not say, I concluded that their observations supported my own." Salm had identified characteristics of the environment that conferred resistance to coral bleaching. He also found characteristics that allowed corals to recover, making them resilient.

Even so, when Salm took his observations to the 9th International Coral Reef Symposium in Bali in October 2000, he was nervous. Here was an august gathering of preeminent marine scientists and coral-reef managers who met only once every four years, and Salm was there to tell them something that seemed so simplistic.

"Rather than being booed off the stage," recalls Salm with a chuckle, "people actually stood up during the meeting and endorsed my observations, saying that they supported their own. And it was heartening to know that they wanted to immediately take this discovery and start using it in the management of their own reefs."

Causey, of the Florida Keys National Marine Sanctuary, heard Salm speak that day. "I had observed over the years that certain coral reefs in the Florida Keys sanctuary had survived the effects of bleaching year after year, and yet these reefs received no special protection," notes Causey. "Rod Salm's hypothesis, I intuitively realized, seemed to provide answers that fit. I felt I could go back to Florida and provide special protection to those areas that could be expected to survive bleaching."

WAVES OF SUPPORT

Since the Bali symposium, conservationists and scientists worldwide have mobilized and integrated their efforts to combat the devastating threat that coral reefs face. For example, Australian researcher William Skirving has been measuring seawater temperatures by satellite and tracking ocean currents on the Great Barrier Reef. He has developed a formula that may predict which reefs are most likely to resist coral bleaching. "Skirving's findings are, potentially, a big breakthrough for coral reef managers," says Marea Hatziolos, team leader for a

World Bank project on the Mesoamerican Barrier Reef supported by the Global Environment Facility. Hatziolos foresees the study helping managers choose marine conservation sites based on the sites' natural resilience to bleaching.

"We believe that our best hope," declares Salm, "is to use the assets nature provides to plan marine protected areas that build resistance to bleaching into their structure." These "refugia," as he calls them, have to be large enough to be self-sustaining and specially protected from overfishing, pollution and siltation. The refugia in turn can reseed coral reefs destroyed by bleaching. "Ultimately," Salm says, "we need to designate these refugia in strategic locations throughout the tropics to create interlinking, mutually sustaining strings of pearls that stretch across our ocean planet."

Between January and April, a huge bleaching event swept through a large part of the Great Barrier Reef, affecting an estimated 60 percent of its corals. This time, with a nod to Salm's hypothesis, conservationists and scientists are planning to turn the disaster into a laboratory experiment. The Australian Institute of Marine Science, collaborating with the Conservancy, will assess the factors associated with resistance to bleaching, specifically testing Salm's observations. Scientists will also begin monitoring coral cover to gauge future effects of bleaching. Furthermore, they will study the genetics of the zooxanthellae, looking for strains that are resistant to bleaching. If any are found, their reefs will be considered as potential refugia, alongside reefs protected by physical factors such as upwellings and currents.

Marine conservation leaders worldwide are embracing new opportunities to save coral reefs. Some have joined with the Conservancy, Conservation International and other groups to implement a coordinated global initiative that aims—in the face of change—to factor resilience into coral reef conservation. Their objective is to work with local groups to create a network of marine protected areas designed to survive, managed to last and connected to one another so as to be mutually sustaining and replenishing. Ultimately, these regional networks, strategically positioned across the tropics, will serve as sanctuaries to the millions of coral reef species whose futures now hang in the balance.

In Palau, plans are already far advanced. Legislation has been moving through Parliament to set up a network of marine protected areas in the archipelago that will serve as a model—the first string of pearls. Collaborating with more than a dozen agencies and community groups, the Conservancy will work to create this series of protected areas using the criteria that Salm discovered on those same reefs a scant two and a half years ago—the first nationwide network of its kind.

"I am optimistic," says Salm. "I think we have discovered a shining beacon of hope for coral reefs. And I, for one, can't wait to make it happen."

Can People Take Too Much From the Oceans?

Just look at a globe and you can see how people might believe that the oceans could provide a limitless supply of anything they want to take from them. Oceans occupy almost three-fourths of Earth's surface, and they are so vast that there are still parts that have not yet been explored. But humans can no longer afford such careless thinking, and new regulations confirm that the government has recognized the dangers of overusing the sea. The 1996 Sustainable Fisheries Act brought the new language of "sustainable yield" into U.S. fishing laws. Now fisheries have to set catch limits that allow different fish species to maintain themselves.[1] An example of why this type of regulation is so necessary can be found in the once-fertile fishing grounds off New England that have been decimated by overfishing. In fact, the whole world has taken notice of how easily ocean life can be destroyed. In 1986, the International Whaling Commission declared a moratorium (suspension of activity) on whaling until the populations of whales recover from decades of overhunting.

In his book *The Empty Ocean*, noted marine researcher Richard Ellis outlines what has happened to our oceans and what is being done to help protect them. The following excerpt from his book identifies the most pressing issues. Since the second part of the 20th century, fishing has become a huge industry. Huge nets, some of them hundreds of miles long, sweep up everything in their paths. Because of the nets' size, fishermen were not catching just the particular type of fish they wanted, like tuna or swordfish, but were wiping out all sea life over enormous areas. Included among the indiscriminate kill, called "by-catch" in the industry, are birds, mammals, sea turtles, and young fish that have not had time to breed—anything that gets in the way of the nets. Some estimates say that by-catch represents 25% of the entire catch. Industrial trawlers, with the sophisticated equipment and huge processing plants on board, can now reach fish in waters a mile deep. As Ellis documents, the numbers of species being unintentionally caught and killed are alarming.

The problems of overfishing are being addressed through legislation, through the development of better fishing practices, and through consumer awareness. It remains to be seen if such measures are being implemented in time to save ocean life, the majority of which has yet even to be identified.

—The Editor

1. Safina, Carl. "The Continued Dangers of Overfishing." *Issues in Science and Technology*. Summer. 2003.

The Empty Ocean
by Richard Ellis

DECLINE OF THE FISHERIES

Abundant signs of the biosphere's limited resilience exist all around. The oceanic fish catch now yields $7.5 billion to the U.S. economy and $82 billion worldwide. But it will not grow further, simply because the amount of ocean is fixed and the organisms it can generate is static. As a result, all of the world's seventeen oceanic fisheries are at or below sustainable yield. During the 1990s the annual global catch leveled off at about 90 million tons. Pressed by ever growing global demand, it can be expected eventually to drop. Already fisheries of the western North Atlantic, the Black Sea, and portions of the Caribbean have collapsed. Aquaculture, or the farming of fish, crustaceans, and mollusks, takes up part of the slack, but at rising environmental cost. This "fin-and-shell revolution" necessitates the conversion of valuable wetland habitats, which are nurseries for marine life. To feed the captive populations, fodder must be diverted from crop production. Thus aquaculture competes with other human activity for productive land while reducing natural habitat. What was once free for the taking must now be manufactured.

—Edward O. Wilson, *The Future of Life*, 2002

The marine ecosystem has traditionally been considered safe from human degradation, mostly because of its size and depth. There was just too much of it for our puny efforts to have much of an effect, and the creatures that lived in it seemed infinite in variety and endless in number. John Seabrook noted in a 1994 *Harper's* magazine article:

> Marine-fishery management has always rested on the assumption that the number of fish in the sea is limitless. Other of our natural resources—timber, bison, land, wild horses—used to be managed in the same way, and each time we neared the end of the resource the philosophy changed. Ocean management has not yet changed, although it has begun to adapt. The ocean is still free, as it has been forever. Traditionally, if you wanted to buy a factory trawler, hire a crew of a hundred men, and go out and catch tens of thousands of fish a day, you didn't have to pay the government anything for the use of the resource—no rent, no special taxes. In fact, the government would help set you up in business with tax incentives and low interest loans.

At his inaugural address to the International Fisheries Exhibition in London in June 1883, Thomas Huxley spoke of the state of the fisheries. Not even a salmon river could be exhausted, he said, because the men who fished the river were "reachable by force of law." That is, they could be restrained by law if the fish population was seen to be threatened. He continued:

> Those who have watched the fisheries off the Lofoden Islands on the coast of Norway say that the coming of the cod in January and February is one of the most wonderful sights in the world; that the cod form what is called a "cod mountain" which may occupy a vertical height of from 20 to 30 fathoms—that is to say, 120 to 130 feet, in the sea, and that these shoals of enormous extent keep coming

in in great numbers from the westward and southward for
a period of something like two months.

On these and other grounds, it seemed to Huxley that "this
class of fisheries—cod, herring, pilchard, mackerel, &c.—might
be regarded as inexhaustible."

In 1961, Hawthorne Daniel and Francis Minot published
The Inexhaustible Sea, a book described on the jacket as "the
exciting story of the sea and its endless resources." But Daniel
and Minot hadn't been reading the newspapers carefully: while
they were writing their book, journalists were reporting that
the anchovy population off the coast of Peru was crashing.
Anchovies (genus *Engraulis*) and sardines (genera *Sardina* and
Sardinops) are among the most important of all commercially
fished species. The California sardine fishery, celebrated
by John Steinbeck in his 1945 novel *Cannery Row*, peaked at
1.5 billion pounds in 1936 but had ceased to exist by 1962.
Anchovetas (*Engraulis ringens*) were so abundant off Peru
Current in such vast numbers that they once headed the list of
largest commercial catches: more than 12.1 million tons were
caught in 1967. But this fishery completely collapsed in 1973
(a result of not only overfishing but also the El Niño of that year),
and the anchoveta, once considered the most numerous fish in
the world, is now greatly reduced in numbers. And the codfish,
responsible for the discovery and early industrial success of
New England, is essentially gone, its "inexhaustible" fishery
closed indefinitely.

At four o'clock every morning of the year, the Tsukiji Fish
Market in Tokyo opens with five acres crammed with sea
life of every description: finfish, sharks, octopuses, squid, sea
urchins, shrimp, lobsters, sea cucumbers, seaweed, and some
things that appear to defy categorization. By ten o'clock,
everything is gone, the market has closed, and workmen are
swabbing the wooden floors of the buildings. Every day, it
looks as if the fishermen have vacuumed another part of
the ocean to fill the market's stalls with an incredible display
of sea life.

The fishermen are fishing as if there were no tomorrow. An article titled "Diminishing Returns" in the November 1995 issue of *National Geographic* begins with these words:

> The unthinkable has come to pass. The wealth of oceans, once deemed inexhaustible, has proven finite, and fish, once dubbed "the poor man's protein," have become a resource coveted—and fought over—by nations.

Even this is an understatement. The fishing off Japan, the decimation of the California sardine fishery, and the crash of the Peruvian anchoveta population are just a few moments in a process that has been going on for decades at an accelerating pace. Throughout the world's oceans, food fishes once believed to be immeasurable in number are now recognized as greatly depleted and in some cases almost extinct. A million vessels now fish the world's oceans, twice as many as there were twenty-five years ago. Are there twice as many fish as before? Hardly.

Close to the precipice of extinction, if not already over the edge, is the white abalone (*Haliotis sorenseni*) of Mexican and California waters. It was said to have occurred in densities of as many as 10,000 individuals per hectare less than half a century ago (a hectare equals 2.47 acres). By the early 1970s, "ab divers" were harvesting these small abalones in substantial quantities because their tender meat made them even more desirable than the larger and tougher pink, red, and green abalones. In 1972, seventy-two tons of white abalone were landed, but after that the catch steadily dwindled; by the early 1990s, the species had virtually disappeared. For almost two years, biologists and divers Gary Davis, Peter Haaker, and Daniel Richards searched areas of "suitable habitat" that were known to have supported this species, and in that time they managed to find only three live individuals, approximately one per acre. "The prognosis for white abalone recovery," wrote Davis and his colleagues in 1996, "is poor, even with immediate active intervention. Wild white abalone broodstock needs to be located quickly and protected, and additional broodstock needs to be produced before significant restoration effort can begin. Population recovery without human intervention is highly unlikely, and white abalone extinction appears imminent." By 1999, the picture had not improved, and in an article titled "Extinction Risk in the Sea," Callum Roberts and Julie Hawkins listed *Haliotis sorenseni* among the soon to be missing. The following year, the National Marine Fisheries Service (NMFS) made it a candidate species under the Endangered Species Act of 1973, and in May 2001, the white abalone became the first marine invertebrate to receive federal protection as an endangered species.

In the past, fish populations were depleted by the simple but lethal expedient of catching too many of the target species, thus reducing the numbers available for future capture and breeding. The introduction of new fishing technologies in the latter half of the twentieth century changed the nature of the industry. Now fishermen deploy longlines that may be a hundred miles long and hung with thousands of baited hooks, which may be intended to catch a particular kind of fish—marlins and swordfish, for example—but catch everything else too, including thousands of unwanted species of fish, sea turtles, dolphins, and seabirds. Drift nets and gill nets sometimes float unattended for years, killing fish and other ocean wildlife that no one will ever harvest. Bottom trawlers scrape the seafloor clean of every living thing, from bottom-dwelling fishes to corals.

No phase of the industry exemplifies "progress" better than the tuna fishery. Once upon a time, tuna of various species were commercially caught on hook and line, with men lined up along the rails of the fishing boats dropping unbaited hooks into a frenzy of feeding tuna, which would snap at anything. The hooked tuna were then yanked from the water, high over the shoulders of the fishermen, and dropped onto the deck. "Their great weight and strength," wrote Robert Morgan (1955), "often make landing by one man with a line impossible . . . and therefore, each hook is operated by two and sometimes three men." In some regions today a similar technique is employed, but the hooks, lines, and jigs are mechanized and there are no fishermen, just a battery of rods bobbing and yanking tuna out of the water and onto the deck.

The biggest change in tuna fishing, however, came with the introduction of the purse seine. Here, a motorboat dispatched from a larger fishing boat encircles a school of tuna with a net, and when the school is completely surrounded, the net, which is closed at the bottom like a colander, is "pursed"—the lines around the top are pulled together—and everything in the mesh is trapped and hauled aboard. Purse seining revolutionized the tuna fishery, particularly in the eastern tropical Pacific, producing catches that dwarfed all previous efforts. But the expeditious capture of albacore and yellowfin tuna had an unexpected downside: for reasons not clearly understood, herds of spinner and spotter dolphins associated closely with the schools of tuna, and when the nets were pursed, the dolphins were trapped too. The term used for the unintentional capture of species not targeted by the fishery is *bycatch*, perhaps the most insidious euphemism in the modern fishing lexicon.

Bycatch refers to the unwanted fish hauled in with the nets, species or sizes that are not marketable—young fish, for example, that have not reached breeding age and thus will never mature and propagate. The term also applies to animals other than fish that are caught in the nets, such as seabirds, dolphins, whales, and turtles. Between June and December 1990, U.S. observers from the National Oceanic and Atmospheric Administration (NOAA) traveling aboard Japanese ships in the northern Pacific sampled 4 percent of the fleet's catch. In addition to catching 7.9 million squid (the target species), seventy-four Japanese vessels took in a bycatch that included 82,000 blue sharks, 253,000 tuna, nearly 10,000 salmonids, 30,000 birds, 52 fur seals, 22 sea turtles, 141 porpoises, and 914 dolphins. Many of these animals are air-breathers; entanglement in fishing nets prevents them from surfacing to breathe, and as a consequence they drown. In the Bering Sea, fishers discarded 16 million undersized red king crabs in 1990—more than five times the number of crabs they were able to bring to market.

The most visible of all bycatches, of course, was the hundreds of thousands of dolphins that were trapped and killed in the tuna nets of eastern tropical Pacific fishermen in the 1960s and 1970s, but this was far from the most harmful and wasteful example. "For every 10 pounds of Gulf of Mexico shrimp scraped from the sea floor," wrote Sylvia Earle in 1995, "80 to 90 pounds of 'trash fish'—rays, eels, flounder, butterfish, redfish, batfish, and more, including juveniles of many species—are mangled and discarded, in addition to tons of plants and animals not even considered worth reporting as 'bycatch,' i.e., starfish, sand dollars, urchins, crabs, turtle grass, seaweed, sponges, coral, sea hares, sea squirts, polychaete worms, horse conchs, and whatever else constitutes the seafloor communities that are in the path of the nets." In a 1996 discussion of the Gulf of Mexico shrimp fishery, NMFS [National Marine Fisheries Service] fishery management specialist Steve Branstetter reported in a similar vein that "shrimp constituted 16% of the total catch by weight, other invertebrates 16%, and finfish 68%." The most abundant species in the bycatch were longspined porgy, brown shrimp, croakers, lizardfish, pink shrimp, and butterfish. Juvenile red snappers made up only 0.4 to 0.5 percent of the total catch by weight, but this percentage was calculated to number between 10 million and 35 million individuals annually, which indicates the incredible extent of the bycatch problem in this region.

With reported landings of 154,083 tons in 1999, shrimp is among the most valuable commercial food fisheries in the United States. According to a statistical database of the Food and Agriculture Organization of the United Nations (FAO), the world's shrimp fisheries hauled in 4,423,673 tons of shrimp and prawns in 1999. If other shrimpers are as efficient as Americans operating in the Gulf of Mexico, that adds as much as 30 million tons—*60 billion pounds*—of wasted fishes, sharks, rays, turtles, starfishes, sea anenomes, and cephalopods (squid and octopuses) that are bycatch in the shrimp fishery.

Stretching as far as a hundred miles, longlines consist of thousands of baited hooks for tuna, swordfish, and other billfishes. But longlines also kill young tuna, swordfish, and marlins that should be allowed to grow and breed, as well as sharks, birds, and other sea life in large quantities. Swordfish can be caught with harpoons, and tuna can be caught with hook and line, but these older ways require more work and are therefore less cost-effective. And if there was ever an industry based on cost-effectiveness, it is the modern fishery. Often marginal, and even more often unprofitable, modern mechanized fisheries are driven to wring every dollar, yen, or kopeck from the sea before the fish populations crash or before interfering legislators make them follow regulations that might actually protect the stocks of fish.

Longline fishing is an especially powerful threat to almost all of the twenty-four recognized living species and subspecies of albatross. Baited hooks are "set" from the rear of the fishing vessel, and before these hooks sink to their optimum fishing depths, the albatrosses dive for the still-floating bait, become hooked, and are dragged underwater and drowned. Each year, the Japanese fishing industry alone sets 107 million or more hooks and is responsible for at least 44,000 albatross deaths. Additional losses are caused by fishing fleets from Argentina, North and South Korea, Indonesia, Uruguay, New Zealand, Taiwan, Peru, Brazil, Hawaii, Namibia, and Australia. At least 60,000 albatrosses and other seabirds may be hooked and drowned by longline fishing vessels engaged in the pirate fishery for Patagonian toothfish, which sets anywhere between 50 million and 100 million hooks in the Southern Ocean each year.

Between 1980 and 1986, the southern bluefin tuna fishery may have accounted for an annual mortality of 2–3 percent of adult wandering albatrosses and 14–16 percent of immature birds nesting on South Georgia Island, in addition to numerous deaths at the Crozet Islands in the South Indian Ocean. It is estimated that as many as 1,500 Tasmanian shy albatrosses, out of a total breeding population of 12,000, are killed each year on longlines. Long-lining contributes to the observed decreases of other albatross populations as well, including the black-footed and Laysan albatrosses of the Northern Hemisphere, especially in the northern Pacific Ocean, the Bering Sea, and the Gulf of

Alaska. In recent years, an estimated 4,500 black-footed alba-trosses have been killed annually by long-line vessels fishing in Hawaiian waters alone. Given the circumpolar distribution of the black-browed albatross and the overlap of its range with fishing efforts, this species may face the greatest threat from fisheries of any albatross. Many of the dead albatrosses (of all species) appear to be inexperienced young birds in their first years of oceanic wandering, which means that the albatrosses lose the young of previous seasons and therefore lose potential breeding adults, leaving a dwindling, aging population. As Carl Safina (2002) pointed out:

> At one time, albatrosses survived extermination only by being at sea. Today, most albatrosses are safe only on land—where they spend just 5 percent of their lives. Hunting and killing on land in decades past was certain to miss at least some islands and some nests and some birds. But nowadays, every albatross, no matter how remote its nest, finds numerous opportunities to die on a longline. If it does and it has a chick on the nest when that happens the chick starves.

There is some cause for hope, however. A new device devel-oped by Ed Melvin and others at the Washington Sea Grant Program could substantially reduce the number of albatrosses caught by long-liners. Each long-liner would be required to fly streamers suspended from strings behind the boat that would flutter in the wind and keep the birds from snatching at the baited hooks. In their 2001 report, Melvin and his colleagues commented, "In 2000, paired streamer lines virtually elimi-nated both Laysan albatross and northern fulmar attacks on baited hooks, and completely eliminated the albatross and northern fulmar bycatch." Safina, in his book titled *Eye of the Albatross: Visions of Hope and Survival*, continues:

> The birds are now reasonably secure on their islands, where once they were hunted mercilessly. The main threat

now comes from longline fishing, but where longline fishing pressure has softened, some albatross populations have begun to trend upward. For example, Wanderer populations on Crozet and Kerguelen Islands in the Indian Ocean, which had plunged by more than half between 1960 and 1990, are now increasing because many longline boats have moved away from these birds' main feeding grounds (after depleting the Southern Bluefin Tuna they'd targeted). Antipodes Albatrosses increased from about eight hundred pairs in the late 1960s to over five thousand pairs by the mid-1990s—by far the greatest increase for any great albatross population. The short-tailed has been increasing at 7 percent per year. Full recovery of these species could still require well over a century, and others are in trouble, but the point is this: these birds were in very bad shape, yet things have changed for the better.

Gill nets, still in common use, are submerged walls of netting whose meshes form a noose around the heads and bodies of fish that swim into them. They are used for surface, midwater, or bottom fishing and can be anchored or set adrift; in the latter case, they are referred to as drift nets. (Drift gill nets, a third type, are attached to the vessel at one end, with the other end drifting behind.) When Japan developed mono-filament fibers that could be used in open-ocean drift-netting in the mid-1970s, it introduced the most destructive method of fishing ever devised. Large-scale high-seas drift nets were first used in the North Pacific by fleets from Japan, Taiwan, and South Korea. Because of the huge bycatch of marine wildlife in these nets, they have been labeled "walls of death"; hundreds of thousands of whales, dolphins, seabirds, sea turtles, sharks, and other nontarget species have been killed by them to date. Free from any connection with the boat, drift nets are set with floats at the top and weights at the bottom so that they drift passively in the water and trap fish that swim into them. Traditionally, these were small nets used in coastal waters to catch densely schooling fish, such as herring, but with the introduction of light synthetic netting, drift net fishing underwent a major change. The nets can now be used on the high seas, where they are very effective at catching wide-ranging species such as tuna and squid. Barely visible in the water, these nets are devastatingly effective at catching all other wildlife in their path. Each boat sets as much as forty miles of net, totaling some *40,000 miles* of drift net, every night—enough to circle the earth one and a half times.

Dolphins and porpoises are probably caught in drift nets because they cannot "see" the monofilament fibers. Even though the dolphins' mechanism of echolocation is incredibly sensitive, the thin strands of fiber that make up the drift net may not reflect sound well enough to provide an echo. And even if the dolphins receive a signal, they may not be echolocating at the moment before entanglement. They may well detect the plastic floats at the tops of the nets, but those would very likely appear to them as no cause for concern, and they certainly give no indication of the danger below. Because most dolphin species are gregarious—none more so than spinners and spotters, which aggregate in huge schools that may number in the thousands—if the "leaders" blunder into a monofilament net, the rest of the school may follow. The long snouts of these dolphins are pushed through the mesh; because the animals are unable to recognize the nature of the snare, they try to push forward and are trapped and drowned.

By 1987, the Japanese squid fleet consisted of more than 1,200 drift netters, each deploying thirty miles of net nightly during a season that lasted seven months. Various conservation organizations, particularly Earthtrust and Greenpeace, campaigned vigorously against this horrifically destructive method, but it would take years of outrage before anything was done. In 1989, videocameraman Sam LaBudde signed on a Panamanian fishing boat as a cook and surreptitiously filmed nets being hauled aboard with dead baby dolphins trapped in the mesh. The film that resulted, *Stripmining the Seas*, became an important weapon in the arsenal designed to bring an end to drift netting. In April 1990, the FAO announced that drift netting had been found even more destructive than previously reported. Between 315,000 and 1 million dolphins of various species, the organization estimated, were being killed annually—in addition to the 20,000 dolphins killed every year in the purse seine fishery for tuna. Although the United States and Japan signed a joint resolution to outlaw drift netting in 1991, Taiwan continued to build drift netters, deploying them off the coast of Africa to avoid detection and prosecution. Under intense international pressure, Taiwan finally shut down its drift net fishery in 1994

The United Nations described large-scale high-seas drift nets as "a highly indiscriminate and wasteful fishing method" and adopted a resolution to ban them. In June 1998, the European Union moved to phase out all drift nets by European nationals and ban the use of drift nets in European waters. Despite this international condemnation, high-seas drift nets continue to kill thousands of dolphins and all manner of other marine life. In January 1999, NOAA banned the use of drift nets by U.S. fishermen in the North Atlantic swordfish fishery to reduce marine mammal bycatch. Because U.S. fishermen are not permitted to use drift nets in the South Atlantic swordfish fishery, this latest ruling bans the use of drift nets in the swordfish fishery throughout the Atlantic Ocean. Drift net fishing for Atlantic swordfish typically involved ten to twelve vessels per year for approximately fourteen days a year, but high bycatch rates of marine mammals and sea turtles prevented a reopening of the fishery.

A method of commercial fishing common in British waters, known as pair trawling, consists of two fishing boats towing a single gigantic net to ensnare fish between them. (Trawling differs from gillnetting in that the trawl is pulled behind a fishing vessel or vessels; gill nets are set and left to fish on their own.) With pair trawling, each vessel pulls on one side of the net, and by carefully coordinating the speed of their boats, the distance between the boats, and the length of their tow wires, the fishermen can precisely control the net's position. The target species is the sea bass, *Dicentrarchus labrax*, a fish that spawns in the Western Approaches, the area of the North Atlantic immediately west of the English Channel. Hundreds of thousands of sea bass gather between December and March every year, and the fry from their spawnings make their way back to the coast in search of sheltered waters in which to feed, grow, and mature. They are particularly fond of estuaries and even more fond of water warmed by the water discharged by nuclear power stations. The young bass are especially vulnerable in these inshore areas; many were being taken before growing big enough to journey back to the Western Approaches to spawn. "Nursery areas" were designated by the British government to give these immature bass some protection, and the number of bass returning to the spawning grounds increased. So many tons of valuable fish in the spawning grounds, however, proved to be too great a temptation, and the large pair trawlers moved in to exploit this otherwise unregulated fishery. French and Scottish pair trawlers had already devastated the black bream fishery for which they had been built, and now they were making massive inroads into the dolphin populations. As many as fifty common dolphins, harbor porpoises, and, occasionally, bottlenose dolphins may be caught in a single haul. Most of the bycatch in this fishery is unreported, but it has been estimated that as many as 2,400 dolphins are killed each year in this process.

Before the advent of industrial fishing, some regions of the ocean were too distant or too deep for fishers to reach, and the fish that lived there remained untouched. But with the introduction of more and more sophisticated gear, no area is safe from human predations. Carl Safina (1998) wrote: "Nowadays, every kind of seabed—silt, sand, clay, gravel, cobble, boulder, rock reef, worm reef, mussel bed, seagrass flat, sponge bottom, or coral reef—is vulnerable to trawling. For fishing rough terrain or areas with coral heads, trawlers have since the mid-1980s employed 'rockhopper' nets equipped with heavy wheels that roll over obstructions." Fishery workers can fish a mile down; they can locate schools of fish whose presence—whose very existence—was unsuspected; they can stay at sea for months and process the catch on board huge factory ships; they can deploy lines that stretch for fifty miles or nets that fish cannot see; they can see the bottom a mile down and drag their huge trawls over it, destroying an entire ecosystem; and they can completely change the character of the food chain.

Fisheries biologist Daniel Pauly is the author of the phrase (and the concept of) *fishing down the food chain*, which means first taking out the apex predators—large species such as cod, tuna, and swordfish—because they are the most desirable species, then, when they are gone, going down a trophic level and taking out their prey species (plankton-eaters such as anchovies), and then taking what's left. This downward shift has occurred as populations of predator fish have been decimated by over-fishing and fishers have been forced to harvest what is left, species of the predators' prey. (From the Greek *trophe*, meaning "food" or "nourishment," *trophic level* refers to the position of organisms within food webs, and ranges from 1 [plant] to 5 [top predators].) To gauge the extent of this shift, researchers have assigned numbers to each trophic level, although the distinctions aren't as clear as one would like, given that many creatures feed at multiple levels. The predators at the very top of the chain, humans, are assigned level 5.0, and piscivorous apex hunters such as tuna and swordfish are assigned level 4.0; then 3.0 is given to the prey of these predators (squid, anchovies, and the like), 2.0 is reserved for the zooplankton (e.g., the copepods on which they feed), and 1.0 denotes the bottom level, the phytoplankton that support the whole struc-ture. "We firmly believe," wrote Pauly and his colleagues in a 2000 *American Scientist* article, "that the mean trophic level of the catch . . . is truly declining":

It takes very little to convince oneself that this situation is alarming—for seafood lovers as well as for environmental-ists. After all, the average trophic level of the global catch has already slipped from 3.4 to 3.1 in just a few decades, and there are not many more appetizing species to be found below this level. [Recall that 2.0 corresponds to copepods and other tiny zooplankton, creatures that are unlikely ever to be filling one's dinner plate.] So if the trend continues, more and more regions are likely to experience complete collapse of their fisheries.

Because the top predators are usually sought first, Robert Steneck, a University of Maine marine biologist, said (1998): "It stands to reason that prey populations and their effects on marine communities will increase after release from predator control. Accordingly, fishing alters the organization and structure of entire marine communities via 'cascading' trophic chain reactions." Because the top predators are the least numerous, as one moves down a food web, biomass increases, but nowadays fish catches have stagnated as fishers have moved from top predators to species at lower trophic levels. Once a top predator has been depleted or exterminated by fishing, alternative predators, which are of no commercial value, thrive in the absence of competition and thus deplete the biomass of prey species at lower trophic levels.

"Fishing down the food chain," of course, is not restricted to human fishers, but the concept is important to an understanding of the ripple effect of overfishing by humans. In Monterey Bay, California, the sea otters were hunted to near extinction, which meant that the sea urchins on which they fed could proliferate unchecked. The urchins in turn gnawed on the holdfasts that anchored the giant kelp, which was thereby cut loose to float on the surface, thus eliminating the entire habitat of the fishes that called these great kelp forests home. When great whales and sea lions began to disappear from Alaskan waters (the whales because they were hunted by humans, the sea lions perhaps because of the removal of pollock, their primary food source), as argued by James Estes of the University of California, Santa Cruz, and colleagues (1998), the killer whales descended one trophic level and began preying on sea otters.

In the northwestern Mediterranean Sea, fishing has depleted sea urchin predators, causing a great increase in the region's dominant sea urchin, *Paracentrotus lividus*, which has grazed the seafloor into "a relatively featureless and largely inedible crustose coralline community." Sea urchins, however, though they might have a low trophic level, filling a niche that has been left vacant by the removal of higher predators, must be recognized as a legitimate part of the marine community, and in some instances the removal of sea urchins has had a calamitous effect on an ecosystem. Around 1983, a still-unidentified pathogen arrived in the western North Atlantic Ocean and began killing off the superabundant sea urchin known as *Diadema antillarum*. The herbivorous *Diadema* kept the reefs clean of "turf algae" and permitted the corals of the Caribbean, the Gulf of Mexico, the Bahamas, and Bermuda to proliferate. When the urchins died, the algae enveloped vast tracts of the underwater landscape, smothering the corals.

The tremendous increase in aquaculture (fish farming) in recent years has been offered as a possible solution to the problems of worldwide overfishing, but aquaculture has its own problems, and in some cases it may be contributing to, rather than solving, the overfishing problem. The species most prominently farmed around the world are carp, salmon, trout, shrimp, tilapia, milkfish, catfish, crayfish, oysters, hybrid striped bass, giant clams, and various shellfish. Of these, shrimp and salmon make up only 5 percent of the farmed fish by weight but almost 20 percent by value. Farming is the predominant production method for salmon, and aquaculture accounts for 25 percent of world shrimp production—a tenfold increase from the mid-1970s.

By a substantial margin, China leads the world in aquaculture, and most of the fish farmed in China are carp, used for regional consumption in low-income households. In other parts of the world, farmed tilapia, milkfish, and channel catfish have replaced depleted ocean fish such as cod, hake, haddock, and pollock. Worldwide landings for the "capture fisheries" (those in which wild fish are caught at sea) have leveled off at around 85–95 million metric tons per year, with most stocks being recognized as fully fished or overfished. In 1990, the figure for aquaculture was 10 million tons, but by 2000 it had nearly tripled. Global aquaculture now accounts for more than one-quarter of all fish consumed by humans.

Each species of farmed fish (shrimp and shellfish are also known as fish in aquaculture-speak) has its own requirements, and it is impossible to generalize about the benefits or detriments of fish farming as a whole. Carnivorous species, such as salmon and shrimp, are usually fed fish meal, made from ground-up fish. The cost of providing food for farmed salmon is nearly as high as the price the salmon can command; moreover, in this case, farming contributes to overfishing because the small fish—such as Peruvian anchovetas—are harvested almost exclusively for fish meal. (It is not only fishes that eat fish meal, of course; most of the processed fish meal is fed to chickens and pigs.) To feed the carnivores, fishermen are fishing for fish to feed to fish.

Carp, tilapia, and milkfish are herbivores and can be fed plant food or prepared fish food not unlike that which hobbyists sprinkle into their home aquariums. Could the vast amount of fishes and other creatures caught incidentally in a particular fishery and usually discarded—the bycatch—be saved and used for fish meal instead of targeted fishery species, such as anchovies? This, unfortunately, would require fishers to use valuable space aboard their ships for storage of bycatch, which are worth less per fish than the expensive fish they are seeking. In a 2001 article on the effects of aquaculture on world fish supplies, Rosamond Naylor (an economist and recognized authority on aquaculture) and two colleagues pointed out:

> Carps and marine molluscs account for more than three-quarters of current global aquaculture output, and tilapia, milkfish and catfish contribute another 5% of total production. Fed mainly on herbivorous diets, these species provide most of the 19 Mt [megatons] gain in fish supplies from aquaculture. . . . But market forces and government policies in many countries favour rapid expansion of high-value, carnivorous species, such as salmon and shrimp. Moreover, fish meal and fish oil are already being added to

carp and tilapia feeds for weight gain, especially in Asia where farming systems are intensifying as a result of increased scarcity and value of land and freshwater resources. Given the huge volume of farmed carp and tilapia in Asia, significant increases in the fish meal and fish oil content of feed could place even more pressure on pelagic [open-ocean] fisheries, resulting in higher feed prices and harm to marine ecosystems.

Shrimp farming is one of the phenomenal success stories in aquacultural history. More than 880,000 tons of shrimp are produced annually from 2.96 million acres of ponds around the world. Annual revenues are estimated to exceed U.S. $6 billion, and the industry is said to be particularly beneficial to developing countries, providing jobs, alleviating poverty, and in some cases even putting food on otherwise barren tables. (Many fishers, however, lost their livelihood.) However, because shrimp farming can be a boom-and-bust phenomenon, environmental and socioeconomic disasters frequently accompany this branch of aquaculture. Shrimp farms often displace home owners, which serves to increase poverty and homelessness; and when rice paddies or mangrove swamps are appropriated for shrimp farms, the net loss to the community cannot be overstated. Ponds located inland often seep saline waters into the surrounding area, which affects the growing of rice and other crops. Aquaculture may provide a long-term solution to the problems of overfishing, but as currently conceived, it often raises more problems than it solves. Here are Naylor and colleagues again:

> Growth in aquaculture production is a mixed blessing, however, for the sustainability of ocean fisheries. For some types of aquaculture activity, including shrimp and salmon farming, potential damage to ocean and coastal resources through habitat destruction, waste disposal, exotic species and pathogen invasions, and large fish meal and fish oil requirements may further deplete wild fisheries stocks.

For other aquaculture species, such as carp and molluscs, which are herbivorous or filter feeders, the net contribution to global fish supplies and food security is great. The diversity of production systems leads to an underlying paradox: aquaculture is a possible solution, but also a contributing factor, to the collapse of fisheries stocks worldwide.

In late 2001, Rosamond Naylor was flying over Sonora looking for shrimp farms, expecting to find "clusters of scattered ponds separated by huge tracts of sere land." Instead, it looked as if the Gulf of California had risen and swept across more than forty-two square miles of the Sonoran Desert: everywhere were "patches of blue, pools of shrimp, one after another, all down the coast," in the words of Marguerite Holloway (2002). Aquaculture, the "blue revolution" of Holloway's article, is by now "a $52 billion-a-year global enterprise involving more than 220 species of fish and shellfish that is growing faster than any other food industry."

We all know that most of the earth is covered with water, but typically we see only the top of it. Beneath its shimmering surface there is a world of life, more intricately woven than that of any rain forest. The occupants range in size from the great whales, the largest animals ever to live on the planet, to microscopic dinoflagellates and submicroscopic viruses. Humans have taken advantage of the ocean's bounty for virtually all of recorded history, probably starting when a prehistoric beachcomber found a dead fish washed ashore, still relatively fresh. From that innocuous beginning or something akin to it, humans became whalers, sealers, aquaculturists, netters, trollers, purse seiners, long-liners, bottom trawlers, rod-and-reelers, dynamiters, poisoners, and myriad others dedicated to removing living things from the ocean. Sometimes the animals were killed for oil, sometimes for baleen, and sometimes for their fur coats, but for the most part they were used for food, and this seemed more than enough justification for the continuing slaughter of the oceans' wildlife. People had to eat, didn't they? Besides, the ocean was so big and so deep and so filled with edible items that there seemed no end to its productivity. If one population of whales (or seals, or fishes, or sharks) was depleted, the fishers simply moved to another area and attacked another population, or changed the object of the fishery. A number of fish species, previously regarded as so plentiful as to be unaffected by human enterprise, have instead shown themselves to be vulnerable to fishing to such a degree that they are now considered endangered. The idea that Mother Ocean would continue to provide for her dependents forever has shown itself to be another gross misjudgment on the part of those dependents.

Rivers, Lakes, and Streams

Why Are Healthy Rivers Important to People?

Throughout human history, entire civilizations have grown around rivers, and entire civilizations have been destroyed when water supplies were lost. How does this happen? Rivers can literally be pumped dry, as happens to the mighty Colorado River as the United States takes about 90% of the river water to meet irrigation and development needs.[1] Mexico uses the remaining 10%, and a trickle reaches the Gulf of California. Sometimes rivers become so polluted that they are of no use for drinking or irrigation, or rivers can be polluted with sediment (soil) from eroded lands. People are becoming more aware of something else about polluted rivers: In addition to the environmental losses, there are heavy financial and social costs that result from misusing them.

The book *Rivers for Life*, written by Sandra Postel and Brian Richter, examines the role of rivers in our world. Sandra Postel is the director of Global Water Policy Project in Amherst, Massachusetts. In November 2002, she was named one of the "Scientific American 50" by *Scientific American* magazine. Brian Richter is director of the Freshwater Initiative of The Nature Conservancy. The following excerpt from their book explores the many reasons we need to protect our river resources. As the authors note, rivers are complex systems that involve food webs, nutrient cycles, wetlands, and countless animal and plant species. Rivers and their wetlands provide clean water and food, help control floods, and provide nutrients to coastal waters. The authors cite some remarkable dollar estimates for the services rivers and their ecosystems provide. But, as they point out, scientists and engineers "have no idea how to re-create many of the more complex processes" river systems perform. So perhaps the lesson goes beyond the financial value of rivers. The strong warning is that we should not destroy something of enormous value that we do not know how to replace.

—The Editor

1. National Aeronautics and Space Administration (NASA). *Earth Observatory*. Available online at *http://earthobservatory.nasa.gov/Newsroom/NewImages/images.php3?img_id=4732*.

Rivers for Life
by Sandra Postel and Brian Richter

THE POLICY TOOLBOX

At a gathering in London in November 2000, former South African president Nelson Mandela captured the essence of the new challenge ahead for societies in their relationships with rivers. The occasion was the release of the final report of the World Commission on Dams, the first-ever independent global review of the effectiveness of large dams in promoting sustainable human development. "It is one thing to find fault with an existing system," Mandela said. "It is another thing altogether, a more difficult task, to replace it with an approach that is better." Surely no one knows this better than Nelson Mandela.

Society's existing approach to managing rivers clearly is not working. Numerous indicators—from the rates of species imperilment, to the decline of fisheries, to the drying up of river flows—show that rivers are at risk. Now that scientists have devised methods of determining how much water a river needs, society is confronted with a clear call to action: will we ensure that those water needs are met?

Many of the conflicts over water use and management that have erupted in recent years reflect the mounting tension between those who wish to heed this call to action and those vested in protecting the status quo. Within the United States, disputes have broken out in recent years over water allocations between "offstream" uses of rivers (e.g., irrigation) and "instream" uses (e.g., protection of endangered species) in the Klamath River basin of California and Oregon; the Snake River basin of Idaho; the Truckee-Carson river system of Nevada; the Apalachicola-Chattahoochee-Flint river basin of Georgia, Alabama, and Florida; and the Shepaug River system of Connecticut—to name just a few. Similar conflicts are arising around the world in river basins large and small, from Southeast Asia's Mekong to South America's Paraguay to southern Africa's Okavango.

Striking a more optimal balance between human water uses and those of rivers themselves will require adjustments. But they need not be wrenching ones, and in the end they will produce a more lasting set of benefits from rivers. A significant portion of society is coming to understand more deeply that human welfare is tightly hitched to the health of the ecosystems around us—that protecting rivers also protects ourselves. Moreover, there is no single, static optimum allocation of water between people and nature. Just as our scientific understanding is evolving about how much water a river needs to be healthy and well-functioning, so is our collective sense about the levels of protection rivers need to be given.

It is now clear, however, that securing the freshwater flows needed to conserve biodiversity and safeguard critical ecosystem services will require governments to reshape laws and policies that were crafted in an earlier time—one concerned with controlling rivers for economic advancement, not with protecting their ecological health for this and future generations. Recasting the rules of river use and management will not be easy. But it is necessary. As Thomas Jefferson wisely observed in 1786, "laws and institutions must go hand in hand with the progress of the human mind.". . .

U.S. POLICY LACKS FOCUS ON ECOLOGICAL HEALTH

With each passing year, the need for greater protection of river flows in the United States becomes more apparent. Two centuries of dam building, levee construction, and straightening of river channels have left very few river segments in anything close to their natural state: only 2 percent of U.S. rivers and streams remain free-flowing. Conflicts over the allocation of water between human needs and ecosystem needs have been intensifying across the country, from west to east and north to south. Freshwater life in running waters is increasingly at risk.

Many western U.S. rivers are oversubscribed, leaving little or no flow to meet ecosystem requirements. Similar signs of stress are apparent now in the eastern portions of the country, areas long thought immune to the water predicaments of the naturally drier West. Nearly 500 kilometers [311 miles] of Vermont's rivers are impaired due to flow alterations and heavy withdrawals. The Ipswich River in Massachusetts now periodically runs dry during the summer months because heavy groundwater pumping for suburban lawn irrigation is depleting the river's base flows. Excessive water withdrawals and diversions have impaired the flow of numerous Connecticut rivers, including the Shepaug, the subject of a citizens suit brought before the state's Supreme Court. In the rapidly growing Southeast, Georgia, Alabama, and Florida have haggled for more than a decade over sharing the waters of the Apalachicola-Chattahoochee-Flint river basin, an ecosystem seriously threatened by rapidly increasing water extractions and flow modifications.

Despite widespread degradation of its river systems, the United States has no overarching vision or goal to secure the flows that rivers need to support the diversity of freshwater life and to sustain ecological functions. Historically, the U.S. government has deferred to the states in matters of water allocation, use, and management. This acquiescence, however, is a matter of choice. The U.S. Constitution makes clear that when state law conflicts with federal, the latter trumps the former. In the area of water allocation, this notion was upheld in the landmark 1899 decision in *United States* v. *Rio Grande Irrigation Co.*, which effectively subordinated state-authorized water uses to federal powers over commerce and public land. According to University of Colorado water-law scholar David Getches, early cases also made it clear that federal preemption of state water law did not require any special legislative action.

In practice, however, federal authorities have rarely interfered with state systems of water rights and allocation, and so the states have called most of the shots. Each state has a body of water law that derives from its constitution, legislative acts, and court decisions. The eastern and western states abide by different legal doctrines, which reflect in part their dissimilar climatic, historical, and economic circumstances. Most eastern states apply the "riparian" doctrine of water law, according to which parties adjacent to rivers and streams can make reasonable use of those waters. Under the riparian system, individuals do not own rights to water. The state permits the use of water bodies, often accompanied by conditions or requirements that ensure such uses do not cause unreasonable harm to others.

By contrast, most western states abide by the "prior appropriation" doctrine, often encapsulated by the motto "first in time, first in right." Those who made the earliest claims on a river have the highest priority rights to its water. Once granted, water rights become the private property of their holder. These rights are what lawyers call "usufructory" rights: they are rights to use water, not to own it outright—hence the other motto that has characterized western water law, "use it or lose it." Along with a specified volume, each water right comes with a date that determines its ranking in the allocation hierarchy. In times of drought, the holder of a more senior water right—one with an earlier date—will get all of his or her water before a more junior rights holder gets any. State agencies administer the applications for and granting of water rights, and any legal challenges are typically handled by state courts.

Federal authorities over rivers take place within the context of these state legal systems. These include federal laws, such as the National Environmental Policy Act (1969), the Clean Water Act (1972), and the Endangered Species Act (1973); case law derived from federal court decisions; as well as authorities granted under the U.S. Constitution, such as the commerce, property, and supremacy clauses. These overlapping and at times competing federal and state authorities would almost certainly not be the policy framework of choice for water management today if, like South Africa, the United States had the opportunity to start over with a blank slate. But it is the system that is in place, and so the challenge lies in interpreting, enforcing, and where necessary, amending these authorities such that they collectively do a better job of balancing human uses of water with the protection of aquatic ecosystems. Our review of the relevant federal and state laws and policies shows a great deal of potential for the protection and restoration of river flows, but most of it so far is unrealized.

FEDERAL OPTIONS

At the federal level, there are at least nine categories of actions or measures that agencies could take to improve river flows. Each of these measures has succeeded in preserving or restoring flows in some cases—establishing all as viable policy tools—but none has been applied broadly enough to significantly improve river flows on a wide scale. Although existing laws and powers seem to give federal agencies the authority to limit flow modifications in order to safeguard river health, this action has not been taken.

The most powerful federal authorities over river flows derive from the commerce clause (Article 1, Section 8) of the U.S. Constitution and the Clean Water Act of 1972. Under the commerce clause, the federal government has the power to regulate commerce among the states and with other nations. Because waters may be used for commercial navigation, it gives Congress some authority over water management. Initially, this authority was interpreted narrowly to cover only activities causing an obstruction to navigable waters. Over time, however, federal courts expanded the definition of "navigable" and the range of activities to which the commerce clause applied. As David Gillilan and Thomas Brown write in their analysis of instream flow protection measures in the western United States, "Eventually the courts determined that rivers did not actually have to be navigable for the Congress to assert its commerce powers. By the time Congress passed the Clean Water Act in 1972, the courts had allowed the federal government to assert jurisdiction over all the waters of the United States, including rivers, lakes, streams, estuaries, and even wetlands."

The federal Clean Water Act (CWA) offers the broadest and clearest mandate to the U.S. Congress to protect river health. Coupled with powers granted under the commerce clause, it leaves little doubt that the federal government has all the authority it needs to protect and restore the flow of rivers. The expressed goal of the act is "to restore and maintain the chemical, physical, and biological integrity of the Nation's waters." During three decades of implementing the act, however,

Congress and the federal agencies administering it have focused primarily on protecting chemical integrity through the setting of water quality standards, pollution control requirements, and best management practices. They have done little explicitly to regulate the quantity and timing of river flows to protect the physical and biological integrity of rivers.

Several events and court decisions during the 1990s extended the reach of the CWA to river flows. So far, however,

Federal Authorities for Protecting River Flows in the United States

ACTION OR MEASURE

➤ Revising management of federal dams built for irrigation, flood control, water supply, hydropower, and navigation

➤ Licensing nonfederal hydropower dams

➤ Listing freshwater species as endangered

➤ Protecting habitat for species listed as endangered

➤ Gaining federal "reserved" water rights through state legal systems

➤ Establishing federal "nonreserved" water rights

➤ Protecting water quality and overall river health

➤ Designating rivers as "wild and scenic"

➤ Controlling activities on public lands that would impact streamflows

PRINCIPAL AGENTS

➤ Army Corps of Engineers

➤ Bureau of Reclamation

these have been relatively isolated cases that demonstrate the act's potential potency but that have so far not led to broader protections. . . .

POWER TOOLS FOR THE STATES

With states effectively having primary responsibility for water allocation and management, they have considerable leverage to secure environmental flows for rivers. As with federal

➤ Department of Energy

➤ Tennessee Valley Authority

➤ Bonneville Power Administration

➤ Western Area Power Administration

➤ Federal Energy Regulatory Commission

➤ Fish and Wildlife Service

➤ Marine Fisheries Service (for salmon)

➤ Secretary of the Interior

➤ All federal agencies impacting rivers

➤ National Park Service

➤ Forest Service

➤ Bureau of Land Management

➤ Indian tribes

➤ Environmental Protection Agency

➤ U.S. Congress

authorities, however, the application of state powers has been patchy, inconsistent, and so far mostly ineffective at protecting the ecological integrity of rivers. Many state efforts still focus on establishing minimum flow requirements, which may keep water running in rivers but not necessarily at the volumes or times that the ecosystems need. Many are also oriented toward safeguarding flows for anglers, boaters, and other recreationists, but not for the ecosystem itself.

A number of policy tools for restoring healthy flows to rivers are available to the states. Although their applicability and practicality vary from state to state, these options include legislating the establishment of environmental flows for rivers, using permit programs to enforce basin-wide limits on flow modifications, granting or transferring water rights for instream purposes, setting conservation goals and requiring conservation programs, and, as legal cases arise, applying judicial protections, such as the public trust doctrine.

The ability most states have to grant, deny, and set conditions on permissions to extract water from state water bodies (often surface water and groundwater) gives them substantial potential to protect river flows. To be used effectively, however, state permitting programs need to be directly keyed to the maintenance of ecological flow regimes such that the sum of all flow modifications in a river do not exceed the threshold defined for that place and time. A "percent-of-flow approach" used by the Southwest Florida Water Management District comes close to this idea. In 1989, the District, which is one of five such geographic districts responsible for managing Florida waters, began limiting direct withdrawals from unimpounded rivers to a percentage of streamflow at the time of withdrawal. For example, cumulative withdrawals from the Peace and Alafia rivers are limited to 10 percent of the daily flow; during periods of very low flow, withdrawals are prohibited completely. The District is now considering using percentage withdrawal limits that vary among seasons and flow ranges in order to better protect the ecological health of rivers under its jurisdiction.

Importantly, this mechanism preserves the natural flow regime of rivers by linking water withdrawals to a percentage of flow—specifically, by ensuring that a major percentage of the natural flow is protected every day. If a new permit application would cause total withdrawals to exceed the threshold, denial of the permit is recommended unless the applicant can demonstrate that the additional withdrawals will not cause adverse ecological impacts. This provision allows for flexibility, but places the burden of proof on potential water users to show that their withdrawals would not harm the ecosystem.

A number of New England states have also taken some positive steps in recent years. In July 2000, Vermont revised its water standards to recognize the need to adjust human-induced flow alterations in order to protect aquatic habitat. The New England office of the U.S. Environmental Protection Agency is working hand in hand with states in the region to encourage the adoption of standards more protective of environmental flows. It has also funded the Connecticut River Joint Commission to examine ways to improve policies affecting flows in the upper Connecticut, New England's largest river.

In western states that apply the doctrine of prior appropriation, the challenge is to establish instream water rights that are sufficient to sustain ecological flows for rivers. None have done this adequately, but many have taken steps either to reserve a portion of flows for instream purposes or, more commonly, to establish minimum streamflows, although these are usually geared toward protecting certain fish species rather than whole ecosystems. Perhaps more importantly, all the western states have criteria for evaluating requests for new appropriative water rights and changes to existing ones, and nearly all (Colorado and Oklahoma are the exceptions) require that new appropriations serve the public interest. Early on, the public interest tended to be equated with economic development, but increasingly public interest criteria are being used to protect river flows from further depletion or modification.

As a result, water rights dedicated to ecosystem protection can now often enjoy the same legal status as rights used for irrigation or other extractive purposes. A major drawback to instream flow water rights designations, however, is that they often have such a low priority date that they do not offer much protection to rivers. To rectify this, some states allocate funds for the purchase of existing higher-priority water rights and then convert them to instream rights. Another important limitation of instream water rights is that they are usually quantified as constant year-round or monthly values that do not come close to approximating a river's naturally variable pattern of flow; they therefore often do little to protect or restore ecosystem health.

One intriguing idea proposed in recent years is that of turning these conventional instream water rights upside down. Instead of prescribing flows for ecosystem support, and implicitly allocating all remaining flows for extractive or other economic purposes, so-called "upside-down instream flow water rights" are defined by turning the question around and asking instead: how much can a river's natural flow pattern be modified in order to meet irrigation, hydropower, and other water development demands and yet still meet the flow needs of the river ecosystem itself? This degree of water development is then specified, and all the remaining flows are allocated to protection of ecosystem functions and services. Attorneys Nicole Silk and Robert Wigington of The Nature Conservancy, along with Jack McDonald of the Northwestern School of Law at Lewis and Clark College, make a strong case for legal recognition of upside-down instream flow water rights either as federally reserved water rights in relation to national parks, forests, or other public lands; or as appropriative rights under state law. These rights may be most applicable, they note, on rivers not overly developed and may work best when implemented with a precautionary approach: that is, reserve only a modest amount of water for development initially, and add more incrementally as scientists develop clearer delineations of where ecological harm will occur.

In essence, upside-down instream flow water rights are a way of implementing the shift toward ecologically compatible water development within the context of the appropriative water rights system in the western United States. In many ways it is similar to the "benchmarking methodology" being applied in parts of Australia. The idea is to permit the withdrawal or modification of only as much flow as the best available scientific evidence can support as unharmful to the river's health. If that threshold is exceeded, then at least society is aware that some degree of ecosystem health is being sacrificed for more water development.

Another underused tool available to the states to protect river flows is their authority (under Section 401 of the federal Clean Water Act) to certify water projects for compliance with state water quality requirements. This authority applies to projects that require a federal license or permit, including hydropower licenses issued by FERC [Federal Energy Regulatory Commission] as well as permits issued by the Army Corps of Engineers for dredging, filling, or altering watercourses or wetlands (under Section 404 of the CWA). Recent court rulings have made clear that states can use this certification authority to powerful effect. In a key 1994 decision (PUD No. 1 of *Jefferson County* v. *Washington Department of Ecology*), the U.S. Supreme Court held that a state could impose flow conditions on a FERC-licensed project if necessary to protect the state's designated uses of the river. The Court swept away any notion that the CWA applies only to water quality and not to water quantity, stating that this is "an artificial distinction," since in many cases "a sufficient lowering of the water quantity in a body of water could destroy all of its designated uses. . . ." The Court said the state of Washington was permitted to set flow requirements in its certification of a hydroelectric facility on the Dosewallips River, because the flows were needed to maintain the designated uses the state had established for the river. . . .

ETHICS IN RIVER POLICY

Do rivers and the life within them have a right to water? In most modern-day legal systems, the answer is no. Water is typically the property of the state, and rights to it are conferred by governments to individuals, cities, corporations, and other human enterprises. Allocations for fish, mussels, and rivers themselves are made only if agents of government deem such allocations socially beneficial, or necessary to fulfill any trust obligations that may exist.

The ethical dimensions of society's water use and management choices could conveniently be ignored as long as those choices did not kill other living things. With freshwater life being extinguished at record rates, however, this is clearly not the case today. Our water management decisions have serious ethical implications, and yet these rarely enter the debate over water plans, projects, and allocations. This may not be surprising given that governments have failed even to provide safe drinking water to all people, which results in several million human deaths each year. Yet our moral obligations both to our fellow human beings and to other life-forms implore us to begin injecting these other ethical implications into our policy choices—to manage water as the basis of life for all living things, rather than as a commodity for the benefit of some.

The fact that rivers have no right to water, and that portions of them maybe held as private property fits into an ethical code grounded in prevailing socioeconomic philosophies, but one that is neither universal nor unchanging. The American conservationist Aldo Leopold viewed the extension of ethics to the natural environment as "an evolutionary possibility and an ecological necessity." More recently, Harvard biologist Edward O. Wilson notes in his book *Consilience* that, historically, ethical codes have arisen through the interplay of biology and culture. "Ethics, in the empiricist view," Wilson observes, "is conduct favored consistently enough throughout a society to be expressed as a code of principles."

In a practical sense, an ethic serves as a guide to right conduct in the face of complex decisions we do not fully understand but that may have serious consequences. Scientists are making clear that the health and life of rivers depend upon a naturally variable flow pattern. As scientists and economists quantify more of the ecosystem services at risk, societies will come to see that the protection of ecosystems is not only an ethical action, but a rational one: acts of stewardship and economic self-interest will converge. But rates of species extinctions and ecosystem decline are too rapid to wait for this convergence to take place. We need some ethical precepts to guide us wisely through this time of risk and uncertainty, and toward actions that preserve rather than foreclose options for this and future generations.

The principle of the public trust offers a good foundation for a code of water ethics in the twenty-first century. Making it a practical guide, however, requires some pragmatic rules and tools. An important one is the ecosystem support allocation, which we have already described in some detail. Another is the precautionary principle, which essentially says that given the rapid pace of ecosystem decline, the irreversible nature of many of the resulting losses, and the high value of freshwater ecosystem services to human societies, it is wise to err on the side of protecting too much rather than too little of the freshwater habitat that remains. It operates like an insurance policy: we buy extra protection in the face of uncertainty.

Applying the precautionary principle to the protection of river health would mean dedicating a large enough share of natural river flows to ecosystem support to accommodate scientific uncertainty over how much water the river system needs. The Benchmarking Methodology that scientists are using to set environmental flow requirements for rivers in Queensland, Australia, takes a precautionary approach by identifying the levels of flow modification beyond which there is increased risk of unacceptable ecological damage. Under Hawaii's new water policies, the state must apply the precautionary principle as a guide for allocating water in fulfillment of its public trust obligations. And in what is perhaps the strongest recognition of the precautionary principle by an international water institution, the International Joint Commission (IJC) adopted it as a guiding principle for protecting the Great Lakes, which straddle Canada and the United States. In a 1999 report to both governments, the IJC cites the precautionary approach as one of five principles, noting: "Because there is uncertainty about the availability of Great Lakes water in the future— . . . and uncertainty about the extent to which removals and consumptive use harm, perhaps irreparably, the integrity of the Basin ecosystem—caution should be used in managing water to protect the resource for the future. There should be a bias in favor of retaining water in the system and using it more efficiently and effectively."

New scientific knowledge about the importance of healthy rivers and the flows required to sustain them has placed upon us new responsibilities. The establishment of ecosystem flow reserves for rivers is essential to protect the diversity of life and to preserve options for future generations. The scientific, legal, policy, and economic tools exist to make these reserves a reality. A basic code of ethics requires that we act.

Is There Enough Freshwater for Both Human Use and the Habitats That Support Plants and Animals?

Here are some numbers to think about. Of all the water on the planet, 97% is in the oceans. About half of the remaining 3% of the Earth's water is frozen in icecaps and glaciers. That leaves a little over 1% of all the water on the planet as available freshwater.[1] Humans take about 50%, or about half, of that small 1% for agriculture, industry, and personal use. But, you might think, there is still half we can use. Well, make a mental list of who else needs that freshwater. Did you remember every plant and animal on the planet? Did you remember all the wetlands, lakes, rivers, and groundwater that support the plants and animals on the planet? Did you remember the oceans that receive daily recharges of water from the rivers running into them?

There is only a fixed amount of water on the planet, a fact that the water cycle demonstrates. Water evaporates, condenses in the clouds, and rains back down—the water you brush your teeth with may once have been used by a dinosaur. With more people on the planet, more water is being taken for human needs from that precious 1% of available freshwater.

We know that people have fought over water for years, but there is a new battle being fought on the planet. In *A Human Thirst*, world-renowned environmental consultant Don Hinrichsen discusses the conflict between humans and habitats, the places in which plants and animals live. He highlights a most striking example—the Aral Sea, located in Uzbekistan and Kazakstan (part of what was once the Soviet Union). It was once the fourth largest inland sea in the world. But because of past Soviet policies to use the water in the rivers that fed it, it has lost three-quarters of its water since the 1960s. Ruined habitat, lost fishing opportunities, and human health dangers are all that are left. As Hinrichsen notes, similar examples challenge the world to launch what he calls a "blue revolution" so that governments can learn to manage water as a sustainable resource. Quite simply, this means not using up all available water until it is gone and everything around the area has died. It is a fact of life that people need a continuous supply of freshwater. In developing a supply that can be sustained, the plants and animals that share the system will benefit also, as will human beings. If we fail, it is not just humans who will suffer the consequences.

—The Editor

1. Smith, Zachary A., and G. Thomassey. *Freshwater Issues*. Santa Barbara: ABC-CLIO, 2002, p. 6.

A Human Thirst
by Don Hinrichsen

Humans now appropriate more than half of all the freshwater in the world. Rising demands from agriculture, industry, and a growing population have left important habitats around the world high and dry.

On March 20, 2000, a group of monkeys, driven mad with thirst, clashed with desperate villagers over drinking water in a small outpost in northern Kenya near the border with Sudan. The Pan African News Agency reported that eight monkeys were killed and 10 villagers injured in what was described as a "fierce two-hour melee." The fight erupted when relief workers arrived and began dispensing water from a tanker truck. Locals claimed that a prolonged drought had forced animals to roam out of their natural habitats to seek life-giving water in human settlements. The monkeys were later identified as generally harmless vervets.

The world's deepening freshwater crisis—currently affecting 2.3 billion people—has already pitted farmers against city dwellers, industry against agriculture, water-rich state against water-poor state, county against county, neighbor against neighbor. Inter-species rivalry over water, such as the incident in northern Kenya, stands to become more commonplace in the near future.

"The water needs of wildlife are often the first to be sacrificed and last to be considered," says Karin Krchnak, population and environment program manager at the National Wildlife Federation (NWF) in Washington, D.C. "We ignore the fact that working to ensure healthy freshwater ecosystems for wildlife would mean healthy waters for all." As more and more water is withdrawn from rivers, streams, lakes and aquifers to feed thirsty fields and the voracious needs of industry and escalating urban demands, there is often little left over for aquatic ecosystems and the wealth of plants and animals they support.

The mounting competition for freshwater resources is undermining development prospects in many areas of the world, while at the same time taking an increasing toll on natural systems, according to Krchnak, who co-authored an NWF report on population, wildlife, and water. In effect, humanity is waging an undeclared water war with nature.

"There will be no winners in this war, only losers," warns Krchnak. By undermining the water needs of wildlife we are not just undermining other species, we are threatening the human prospect as well.

PULLING APART THE PIPES

Currently, humans expropriate 54 percent of all available freshwater from rivers, lakes, streams, and shallow aquifers. During the 20th century water use increased at double the rate of population growth: while the global population tripled, water use per capita increased by six times. Projected levels of population growth in the next 25 years alone are expected to increase the human take of available freshwater to 70 percent, according to water expert Sandra Postel, Director of the Global Water Policy Project in Amherst, Massachusetts. And if per capita water consumption continues to rise at its current rate, by 2025 that share could significantly exceed 70 percent.

As a global average, most freshwater withdrawals— 69 percent—are used for agriculture, while industry accounts for 23 percent and municipal use (drinking water, bathing and cleaning, and watering plants and grass) just 8 percent.

The past century of human development—the spread of large-scale agriculture, the rapid growth of industrial development, the construction of tens of thousands of large dams, and the growing sprawl of cities—has profoundly altered the Earth's hydrological cycle. Countless rivers, streams, floodplains, and wetlands have been dammed, diverted, polluted, and filled. These components of the hydrological cycle, which function as the Earth's plumbing system, are being disconnected and plundered, piece by piece. This fragmentation has been so extensive that freshwater ecosystems are perhaps the most severely endangered today.

Consider the plight of wetlands—swamps, marshes, fens, bogs, estuaries, and tidal flats. Globally, the world has lost half of its wetlands, with most of the destruction having taken place over the past half century. The loss of these productive ecosystems is doubly harmful to the environment: wetlands not only store water and transport nutrients, but also act as natural filters, soaking up and diluting pollutants such as nitrogen and phosphorus from agricultural runoff, heavy metals from mining and industrial spills, and raw sewage from human settlements.

In some areas of Europe, such as Germany and France, 80 percent of all wetlands have been destroyed. The United States has lost 50 percent of its wetlands since colonial times. More than 100 million hectares of U.S. wetlands (247 million acres) have been filled, dredged, or channeled—an area greater than the size of California, Nevada, and Oregon combined. In California alone, more than 90 percent of wetlands have been tilled under, paved over, or otherwise destroyed.

Destruction of habitat is the largest cause of biodiversity loss in almost every ecosystem, from wetlands and estuaries to prairies and forests. But biologists have found that the brunt of current plant and animal extinctions has fallen disproportionately on those species dependent on freshwater and related habitats. One fifth of the world's freshwater fish—2,000 of the 10,000 species identified so far—are endangered, vulnerable, or extinct. In North America, the continent most studied, 67 percent of all mussels, 51 percent of crayfish, 40 percent of amphibians, 37 percent of fish, and 75 percent of all freshwater mollusks are rare, imperiled, or already gone.

The global decline in amphibian populations may be the aquatic equivalent of the canary in the coal mine. Data are scarce for many species, but more than half of the amphibians studied in Western Europe, North America, and South America are in a rapid decline.

Around the world, more than 1,000 bird species are close to extinction, and many of these are particularly dependent on wetlands and other aquatic habitats. In Mexico's Sonora Desert, for instance, agriculture has siphoned off 97 percent of the region's water resources, reducing the migratory bird population by more than half, from 233,000 in 1970 to fewer than 100,000 today.

Left High and Dry

Habitat destruction, water diversions, and pollution are contributing to sharp declines in freshwater biodiversity. One-fifth of all freshwater fish are threatened or extinct. On continents where studies have been done, more than half of amphibians are in decline. And more than 1,000 bird species—many of them aquatic—are threatened. More than 40,000 large dams bisect waterways around the world, and more than 500,000 kilometers of river have been dredged and channelized for shipping. Deforestation, mining, grazing, industry, agriculture, and urbanization increase pollution and choke freshwater ecosystems with silt and other runoff. Water diversion for irrigation, industry, and urban use has increased 35-fold in the past 300 years. In some cases, this increased demand has deprived entire ecosystems of water. Sprawl is an increasing concern, as the spread of urban areas is destroying important wetlands, and paved-over area is reducing the amount of water that is able to recharge aquifers.

Pollution is also exacting a significant toll on freshwater and marine organisms. For instance, scientists studying beluga whales swimming in the contaminated St. Lawrence Seaway, which connects the Atlantic Ocean to North America's Great Lakes, found that the cetaceans have dangerously high levels of PCBs in their blubber.

In fact the contamination is so severe that under Canadian law the whales actually qualify as toxic waste.

Waterways everywhere are used as sewers and waste receptacles. Exactly how much waste ends up in freshwater systems and coastal waters is not known. However, the UN Food and Agriculture Organization (FAO) estimates that every year roughly 450 cubic kilometers (99 million gallons) of wastewater (untreated or only partially treated) is discharged into rivers, lakes, and coastal areas. To dilute and transport this amount of waste requires at least 6,000 cubic kilometers (1.32 billion gallons) of clean water. The FAO estimates that if current trends continue, within 40 years the world's entire stable river flow would be needed just to dilute and transport humanity's wastes.

THE POINT OF NO RETURN?

The competition between people and wildlife for water is intensifying in many of the most biodiverse regions of the world. Of the 25 biodiversity hotspots designated by Conservation International, 10 are located in watershort regions. These regions—including Mexico, Central America, the Caribbean, the western United States, the Mediterranean Basin, southern Africa, and southwestern China—are home to an extremely high number of endemic and threatened species. Population pressures and overuse of resources, combined with critical water shortages, threaten to push these diverse and vital ecosystems over the brink. In a number of cases, the point of no return has already been reached.

CHINA

China, home to 22 percent of the world's population, is already experiencing serious water shortages that threaten both people and wildlife. According to China's former environment minister, Qu Geping, China's freshwater supplies are capable of sustainably supporting no more than 650 million people—half its current population. To compensate for the tremendous shortfall, China is draining its rivers dry and mining ancient aquifers that take thousands of years to recharge.

As a result, the country has completely overwhelmed its freshwater ecosystems. Even in the water-rich Yangtze River Basin, water demands from farms, industry, and a giant population have polluted and degraded freshwater and riparian ecosystems. The Yangtze is one of the longest rivers in Asia, winding 6,300 kilometers [3,915 miles] on its way to the Yellow Sea. This massive watershed is home to around 400 million people, one third of the total population of China. But the population density is high, averaging 200 people per square kilometer. As the river, sluggish with sediment and laced with agricultural, industrial, and municipal wastes, nears its wide delta, population densities soar to over 350 people per square kilometer.

The effects of the country's intense water demands, mostly for agriculture, can be seen in the dry lake beds on the Gianghan Plain. In 1950 this ecologically rich area supported over 1,000 lakes. Within three decades, new dams and irrigation canals had siphoned off so much water that only 300 lakes were left.

China's water demands have taken a huge toll on the country's wildlife. Studies carried out in the Yangtze's middle and lower reaches show that in natural lakes and wetlands still connected to the river, the number of fish species averages 100. In lakes and wetlands cut off and marooned from the river because of diversions and drainage, no more than 30 survive. Populations of three of the Yangtze's largest and most productive fisheries—the silver, bighead, and grass carp—have dropped by half since the 1950s.

Mammals and reptiles are in similar straits. The Yangtze's shrinking and polluted waters are home to the most endangered dolphin in the world—the Yangtze River dolphin, or Baiji. There are only around 100 of these very rare freshwater dolphins left in the wild, but biologists predict they will be gone in a decade. And if any survive, their fate will be sealed when the massive Three Gorges Dam is completed in 2013. The dam is expected to decrease water flows downstream, exacerbate the effects of pollution, and reduce the number of prey species that the dolphins eat. Likewise, the Yangtze's Chinese alligators, which live mostly in a small stretch near the river's swollen, silt-laden mouth, are not expected to survive the next 10 years. In recent years, the alligator population has dropped to between 800 and 1,000.

THE ARAL SEA

The most striking example of human water demands destroying an ecosystem is the nearly complete annihilation of the 64,500 square kilometer [24,904-square-mile] Aral Sea, located in Central Asia between Kazakhstan and Uzbekistan. Once the fourth largest inland sea in the world, it has contracted by half its size and lost three-quarters of its volume since the 1960s, when its two feeder rivers—the Amu Darya and the Syr Darya—were diverted to irrigate cotton fields and rice paddies.

The water diversions have also deprived the region's lakes and wetlands of their life source. At the Aral Sea's northern end in Kazakhstan, the lakes of the Syr Darya delta shrank from about 500 square kilometers [193 square miles] to 40 square kilometers [15 square miles] between 1960 and 1980. By 1995, more than 50 lakes in the Amu Darya delta had dried up and the surrounding wetlands had withered from 550,000 hectares [1.4 million acres] to less than 20,000 hectares [49,421 acres].

The unique *tugay* forests—dense thickets of small shrubs, grasses, sedges and reeds—that once covered 13,000 square kilometers [5,019 square miles] around the fringes of the sea have been decimated. By 1999 less than 1,000 square kilometers [386 square miles] of fragmented and isolated forest remained. The habitat destruction has dramatically reduced the number of mammals that used to flourish around the Aral Sea: of 173 species found in 1960, only 38 remained in 1990. Though the ruined deltas still attract waterfowl and other wetland species, the number of migrant and nesting birds has declined from 500 species to fewer than 285 today.

Plant life has been hard hit by the increase in soil salinity, aridity, and heat. Forty years ago, botanists had identified 1,200 species of flowering plants, including 29 endemic species. Today, the endemics have vanished. The number of plant species that can survive the increasingly harsh climate is a fraction of the original number.

Alien Invaders

"Rapidly growing populations place heavy demand on freshwater resources and intensify pressures on wildlands," concludes a combined World Resources Institute and Worldwatch report called "Watersheds of the World." But increasingly, the introduction of exotic or alien species is playing a large role in wreaking havoc on freshwater habitats. The spread of invasive species is a global phenomenon, and is increasingly fostered by the growth of aquaculture, shipping, and commerce. Whether introduced by accident or on purpose, these alien invaders are capable of altering habitats and extirpating native species en masse. The invasion and insidious spread of the zebra mussel in the U.S. Great Lakes highlights the tremendous costs to ecosystems and species. A native of Eastern Europe, the zebra mussel arrived in the Great Lakes in 1988, released most likely through the discharge of ballast waters from a cargo ship. Once established, it spread rapidly throughout the region.

The mussels have crowded out native species that cannot compete with them for space and food. A study of the mussels in western Lake Erie found that all of the native clams at each of 17 sampling stations had been wiped out. Moreover, the last known population of the winged maple leaf clam, found in the St. Croix River in the upper Mississippi River basin, is now threatened by advancing ranks of the zebra mussel.

Most experts agree that the sea itself may very well disappear entirely within two decades. But the region's freshwater habitats and related communities of plants and animals have already been consigned to oblivion.

LAKE CHAD

Lake Chad, too, has shrunk—to one-tenth of its former size. In 1960, with a surface area of 25,000 square kilometers [9,653 square miles], it was the second-largest lake in Africa. When last surveyed, it was down to only 2,000 square kilometers [772 square miles]. And here, too, massive water withdrawals from the watershed to feed irrigated agriculture have reduced the amount of water flowing into the lake to a trickle, especially during the dry season.

Lake Chad is wedged between four nations: populous Nigeria to the southwest, Niger on the northwest shore, Chad to the northeast, and Cameroon on a small section of the south shore. Nigeria has the largest population in Africa, with 130 million inhabitants. Population-growth rates in these countries average 3 percent a year, enough to double human numbers in one generation. And population growth rates in the regions around the lake are even higher than the national averages. People gravitate to this area because the lake and its rivers are the only sources of surface water for agricultural production in an otherwise dry and increasingly desertified region.

Although water has been flowing into the lake from its rivers over the past decade, the lake is still in serious ecological trouble. The lake's fisheries have more or less collapsed from over-exploitation and loss of aquatic habitats as its waters have been drained away. Though some 40 commercially valuable species remain, their populations are too small to be harvested in commercial quantities. Only one species—the mudfish—remains in viable populations.

As the lake has withered, it has been unable to provide suitable habitat for a host of other species. All large carnivores, such as lions and leopards, have been exterminated by hunting and habitat loss. Other large animals, such as rhinos and hippopotamuses, are found in greatly reduced numbers in isolated, small populations. Bird life still thrives around the lake, but the variety and numbers of breeding pairs have dropped significantly over the past 40 years.

A BLUE REVOLUTION

As these examples illustrate, the challenge for the world community is to launch a "blue revolution" that will help governments and communities manage water resources on a more sustainable basis for all users. "We not only have to regulate supplies of freshwater better, we need to reduce the demand side of the equation," says Swedish hydrologist Malin Falkenmark, a senior scientist with Sweden's Natural Science Research Council. "We need to ask how much water is available and how best can we use it, not how much do we need and where do we get it." Increasingly, where we get it from is at the expense of aquatic ecosystems.

If blindly meeting demand precipitated, in large measure, the world's current water crisis, reducing demand and matching supplies with end uses will help get us back on track to a more equitable water future for everyone. While serious water initiatives were launched in the wake of the World Summit on Sustainable Development held in Johannesburg, South Africa, not one of them addressed the water needs of ecosystems.

There is an important lesson here: just as animals cannot thrive when disconnected from their habitats, neither can humanity live disconnected from the water cycle and the natural systems that have evolved to maintain it. It is not a matter of "either or" says NWF's Krchnak. "We have no real choices here. Either we as a species live within the limits of the water cycle and utilize it rationally, or we could end up in constant competition with each other and with nature over remaining supplies. Ultimately, if nature loses, we lose."

By allowing natural systems to die, we may be threatening our own future. After all, there is a growing consensus that natural ecosystems have immense, almost incalculable value. Robert Costanza, a resource economist at the University of Maryland, has estimated the global value of freshwater wetlands, including related riverine and lake systems, at close to $5 trillion a year. This figure is based on their value as flood regulators, waste treatment plants, and wildlife habitats, as well as for fisheries production and recreation.

The nightmarish scenarios envisioned for a waterstarved not too distant future should be enough to compel action at all levels. The water needs of people and wildlife are inextricably bound together. Unfortunately, it will probably take more incidents like the one in northern Kenya before we learn to share water resources, balancing the needs of nature with the needs of humanity.

Why Does the Federal Government Want to Save the Everglades, the Largest Freshwater Marsh in the United States?

In 1947, some people had the foresight to create Everglades National Park in southern Florida. Today, this "river of grass" is the largest subtropical wilderness in the country.[1] In recognition of its importance to the world, it has also been designated as an International Biosphere Reserve, a World Heritage Site, and a Wetland of International Importance. But the Everglades of 1947 has changed in what many consider a frightening way. More than 50 years of pollution, of diverting water into the ocean to drain the land, of straightening its rivers into channels and canals, and of losing over half the land to agriculture and development, have caused great damage. There is a growing number of endangered and threatened species in the Everglades: the Florida panther, the manatee, the American crocodile, and the wood stork, to name just a few.

In 2000, the U.S. government responded to this crisis with a plan. The plan is impressive, just like the Everglades it seeks to restore and to protect. It is called the Comprehensive Everglades Restoration Plan (CERP), has a $7.8 billion price tag, and a 30-year timetable.[2] The plan involves more than 70 different projects. In June 2004, it was announced that the National Academy of Sciences, one of the nation's most prestigious scientific groups, would act as an independent review panel for CERP.[3]

The conservation issue of the Everglades is water: who gets it, when do they get it, and what will keep it from being polluted. Everglades plants and animals are adapted to the natural wet and dry cycles of the seasons flowing over the natural landscape carved out by the once meandering Kissimmee River. It remains to be seen whether putting water back into an area that has been physically reshaped to meet human development needs will work ecologically. But, at the very least, the tide has turned from

116

destroying the wetland to trying to restore and protect the magnificent biodiversity of this national, and, indeed, world, treasure.

—The Editor

1. Douglas, Margery Stoneman. *The Everglades: River of Grass*. Florida: Pineapple Press, 1997.

2. The Comprehensive Everglades Restoration Plan (CERP). United States Geological Survey. 2004. Available online at *http://fl.water.usgs.gov/CERP/cerp.html*.

3. News Release No. PA-04-12. June 14, 2004. U.S. Army Corps of Engineers.

"Reviving a River of Grass"
by Ted Levin

Sitting on the bow of an airboat, 15 miles from the nearest road, I watch mist rising off the leafy marsh. Sawgrass extends to the horizon, broken only by a few islands of green and by shallow braids of water, where lilies and bladderworts bloom in the heat. Angry clouds pile up to the south, while in the east, beyond the early-morning congestion of Fort Lauderdale, shafts of yellow sunlight rake the sky. It's late April, the tip of a new day, and the tip of a new season in the Florida Everglades.

It's also a new beginning for one of the world's grandest and most beleaguered wetlands, now on the cusp of perhaps the largest ecological restoration ever undertaken. The Comprehensive Everglades Restoration Plan will cost nearly $8 billion and take almost half a century to complete, and even then there are a multitude of uncertainties that could derail it along the way. But every one of the dozens of scientists who had a hand in shaping the plan agrees on one thing: It couldn't have come any sooner.

In essence, the plan's main objective is to recapture as much as 1.7 billion gallons of the fresh water currently being flushed out to sea every day and redirect that water back to the ailing wetlands—all without flooding South Florida's farms and booming cities. For years the Everglades ecosystem, which stretches from Orlando to the Florida Keys, has been on the brink of ecological collapse. Its unique mosaic of sawgrass marshes, wet prairies, sloughs, and hardwood swamps has been drained and diked over the past hundred years, rendering the landscape habitable for people but untenable for panthers, egrets, crocodiles, and dozens of other Everglades-dependent species. The disruption of seasonal water flows has wreaked havoc on the ecosystem's delicate balance. In addition, invasive species are replacing natives at a rapid pace, and phosphorus runoff from agriculture has severely diminished water quality. Wildlife has taken the greatest hit: Fish numbers have dropped precipitously, and populations of nesting wading birds such as wood storks and white ibis have plummeted by more than 90 percent in the past 50 years.

The $7.8 billion restoration, which is made up of nearly 70 different projects, has many scientists believing they can reverse this decline. Still, no one is guaranteeing success. "Our understanding of the Everglades is based almost entirely on information collected after it became a disturbed ecosystem," says John Ogden, a senior ecologist for the South Florida Water Management District, one of the agencies carrying out the restoration. "We don't know what the natural system really is, so we're basing these projects on a set of predictions on how we think it will respond."

The good news is that the restoration will eliminate some 240 miles of canals and levees, thus allowing for more natural flows of water to course through the River of Grass. The plan also calls for the construction of new filtering marshes that will cleanse the runoff from 700,000 acres of farms and sugarcane fields, as well as artificial reservoirs and underground water-storage facilities designed to ensure a steady supply of water for South Florida's thirsty residents. The water stored in the reservoirs and underground aquifers is to be released periodically, to mimic the historical wet-dry cycle.

The bad news is that no one knows if any of this will really work—whether the wildlife will actually rebound and whether the 300 wells drilled 1,000 feet underground will be able to hold much of the water that is now being shunted out to the Atlantic Ocean and the Gulf of Mexico. What scientists do admit is that there are no ironclad guidelines for the restoration; some of the technology will have to be worked out along the way. "Maybe it's premature to implement a plan," says Stuart Applebaum, chief of ecosystem restoration in the U.S. Army Corps of Engineers' Jacksonville office. "But the Everglades is in dire straits, and I don't want to do a postmortem."

Historically, nearly everything south of Disney World was covered by a low-lying, seasonally flooded wetland; the Everglades ecosystem itself was more than 60 miles wide and so shallow that a grown man could walk across it without getting his hair wet (unless he got mired in the peat, the soil formed from decaying plants). The wide floodplains of the Everglades— called marl prairies, and as slick as grease when they're wet— were flooded and dried every year. During wet periods, when the sloughs spilled over their banks and flooded the limy, rock-studded earth, the prairies became a biological mecca; every winter the fish marooned in drying potholes and depressions attracted thousands of wading birds.

To seed the clouds that bring rain to the Everglades, there must be thousands of square miles of water that moves almost imperceptibly; then the sun pulls the water back to the sky, where it forms new clouds. Nothing in South Florida, however, is less predictable than the weather. Florida gets about 55 inches of rain a year. On average, three-quarters of that rainfall occurs during the wet season—from June to October—but the seam between the seasons is periodically obliterated by multiyear cycles of flood and drought.

Anything that lives in the Everglades must tolerate these swings; some life-forms rely on them. The seeds of sawgrass and cypress, for example, germinate primarily on dry ground, even though the plants themselves can survive a year or more of inundation. The unpredictability of South Florida's weather places the snail kite—a red-legged, crow-size hawk—and the robust wood stork at opposite ends of this meteorological see-saw. The annual wet season and prolonged periods of flood are good for the kites, which eat snails that live in permanently flooded marshes. The annual dry season and prolonged periods of drought are good for the wood storks, which gorge on fish concentrated in the shrinking pools. Who could imagine a more unusual system than one that supports two species of birds that depend on such divergent meteorological swings?

Not the Army Corps of Engineers, which in 1948 began a massive flood-control project to tame the sodden landscape. A year earlier torrential rains had dumped about 10 feet of water on the Everglades, flooding most of South Florida, including much of Miami. The outcry from citizens and farmers prompted a call to arms; during the next three decades the Corps constructed an elaborate network of more than 1,600 miles of canals and levees that subdivided the Everglades into an agricultural district, three water-conservation areas, and a national park. The Corps' engineers straightened the Kissimmee River, one of the main sources of water in the Everglades ecosystem, transforming it from a curving, 105-mile-long waterway into a 56-mile-long canal; they also dredged and widened the Caloosahatchee River, which diverts Everglades water to the Gulf of Mexico.

For the millions who have flocked to the Sunshine State in the past 50 years, the plan has worked marvelously; for the region's plants and animals, 68 species of which are either federally or regionally endangered or threatened, it's been a disaster. "Unfortunately, they built a system that can't deal with those ecological extremes inherent to the Everglades," says Ogden. To provide both flood protection and a steady supply of drinking water for South Florida's 6 million residents, natural resource managers are forced to store excess water in the conservation areas—affording those areas little chance for a natural dry-down cycle. As a result, parts of both the northern and the southern Everglades remain bone dry, and for unnaturally long periods. Muck fires, triggered by lightning strikes in the unusually dry conditions, have devastated large swaths of the wetlands. In total, many areas of the Everglades are either drowning or burning, and the national park—at the southern tip—is on life support. "What we have out there now is Everglades in name only," says Ogden. "It may look like the Everglades, but it doesn't function like the Everglades."

During the last decades of the 19th century, before the demands of the feather trade crippled Florida's wading-bird populations, some biologists speculated that as many as 1.5 million of the birds nested in the mangrove-lined rivers at the southern end of Everglades National Park. Ogden thinks that number may be inflated. The high-end estimate he favors is 250,000—most of them white ibis—a number recorded in both the 1933 and 1934 breeding seasons by the Audubon Society wardens whose job it was to patrol the waterlogged backcountry during the first half of the past century (something the state of Florida was loath to do).

Today the mangrove rookeries stand empty and silent in testimony to engineering gone awry. Populations of wood storks and white ibis, both tactile feeders, and snowy egrets, immaculate little herons that comb the shallows as if they were wired on caffeine, have crashed or moved elsewhere. To accommodate populations of the federally endangered wood stork and snail kite, ecological restoration must re-create capricious wetlands, which are routinely enriched by yearly cycles of wet and dry punctuated by extended drought and violent flood.

Alligators, a keystone species whose excavations once attracted a jubilee of aquatic life to the marl prairies, have substantially redistributed themselves. When normally wet areas are deprived of water, the gators are forced to move off the marl edges and into the much deeper central Everglades, where prey is hard to come by. Today the marl prairies, where the alligators once ruled, are mostly barren of life. But, says Ogden, if these rich prairies can once again become suitable for alligators, "then we've gone a long way toward restoration."

Because water cues the nesting and distribution of wading birds, alligators, and snail kites, and many lesser-known species, too, ecologists hope the replumbed system will once again become a wildlife version of the movie *Field of Dreams:* If you water it, they will come.

But scientists are split on exactly how much water should be put back into the Everglades. One camp, which consists mostly of biologists and hydrologists from Everglades National Park, insists that anything less than 80 percent of historical water flows will be insufficient to kick-start the ecosystem on the road back to health. The current plan calls for only about 70 percent of those flows to be spread out across the Everglades. "But it isn't as if you get 70 percent of the ecological functions back with 70 percent of the water," says Tom Van Lent, a hydrologist with Everglades National Park. Based on computer modeling, park scientists have determined that 80 to 90 percent of the historical water volume is the amount necessary to trigger conditions that would be favorable to the marl prairies, the southern estuaries, and nesting wading birds.

Other scientists, mostly from the U.S. Army Corps of Engineers and the South Florida Water Management District, contend that less water will be adequate, as long as certain depths are restored in most of the decimated parts of the ecosystem. Given that half of the original Everglades has been swallowed up by houses and sugarcane, these scientists say the Everglades ecosystem can't even absorb the same amount of water it held a hundred years ago. Recent studies by the Environmental Protection Agency, which reveal substantial peat loss in the drier parts of the Everglades, seem to back up this claim. "Our information shows that these areas have lost 39 to 69 percent of their soil," says Dan Scheidt, a senior scientist with the EPA.

The construction of levees and the flatter landscape—brought on by the loss of peat—changes the whole water equation, says Lorraine Heisler, a biologist with the U.S. Fish and Wildlife Service. "We can put all the water back in there, but with a different topography we're not going to have the same watershed," she says. "It's like restoring a river in a different channel." The impact of the extra water would be greatest on the central Everglades, where a significant percentage of the tree islands—wooded habitats in the marshes that took more than a thousand years to develop and that are stressed by the unnaturally deep water—have already drowned.

"Restoring historic sheet flow is desirable but not every-where possible," concurs Ogden, "particularly with today's water quality being what it is in the Everglades." In fact, agri-cultural runoff is considered the 800-pound gorilla lurking in the background. New water-quality standards have reduced the amount of phosphorus being pumped into the marshes, but there is still plenty getting spewed out, and those 700,000 agricultural acres sitting near the top of the ecosystem aren't going anywhere in the foreseeable future. "From a scientific point of view," Ogden adds, "pumping extra water into the Everglades can cause as many problems as it solves, especially if that water isn't clean enough, or if it floods tree islands." Nonetheless, the park's concerns have not gone unheeded: Officials from the Army Corps of Engineers have agreed to consider adding an extra 250,000 acre-feet of water to the restoration plan, which park biologists say will get them closer to that 80 to 90 percent figure.

What the Everglades needs is a King Solomon to consider all the water politics and tease out all the trade-offs. "Everyone wants their piece of the system to be fixed right now," says Robert Pace, a biologist with the U.S. Fish and Wildlife Service. "But it's not easy to please everyone." In the end, success will be measured by how well the ecosystem and all its creatures bounce back. Ecologists will be looking to see if healthy popu-lations of fish and wading birds and alligators can be sustained, if exotic vegetation can be eliminated, and if tree islands can be restored as havens of biodiversity. Then, after the slow creep of time, would come the building of peat. "We won't be able to return the Everglades to the way it looked in 1850," says Heisler, "but we'll be successful if we can restore the ecological vibrancy that allows wildlife and birds to flourish."

Back on the airboat, under a wide sky and a blazing sun, I close my eyes and imagine that it's late January 2050—about a dozen years after the target completion date for the Everglades restoration. Shoals of tiny fish gather in depressions on the marl prairies, waiting. Tens of thousands of puddles. Millions of fish. Day by day, the pools shrink, and the fish—mostly

mosquito fish, marsh killifish, least killifish, sailfin mollies—
wait for death, impaled by the lances of the sun or speared by
the squadrons of birds that I picture gathering here each morning. Along the apron of the Everglades, time has always been
measured by the presence or absence of water. Here, it's the
middle of the dry season, and this bumper crop of ill-fated fish,
crayfish, and grass shrimp, which are themselves three or four
years in the making, may well trigger one of North America's
most awesome pageants: a convocation of wading birds.

Can We Protect the Wildlife and Habitat Around Yellowstone National Park?

Yellowstone National Park, the world's first national park, is home to many things. It is home to Old Faithful and other amazing geysers. It is home to grizzlies, wolves, elk, cougars, coyotes, and bison—the largest concentrations of hoofed wildlife and large predators in the continental United States. The park sounds like it has a lot of land—2.2 million acres. But the 1872 original park boundaries were drawn to include the geysers, not to meet the habitat needs of the animal residents. Therefore, Yellowstone Park is also home to some controversial conservation issues.

William Stolzenburg is the editor of *The Nature Conservancy* magazine. His 2003 article, "The Lone Rangers," explores what to do about the animals that don't know they are supposed to stay inside their "2.2 million acre zoo." Scientists are now considering trying to protect a larger area called the Greater Yellowstone Ecosystem, about 25 million acres that would safeguard the area's great biodiversity. The site was first identified by biologists as the land needed to sustain Yellowstone's population of grizzly bears. Now it has grown to include the ecosystem needed to protect the 1,600 native species found in the park. As recent wolf sightings in Utah have shown, wolves travel across state boundaries in search of new territories and mates. Grizzlies can roam up to 360 square miles in a year. At issue is that people who live in the area around Yellowstone. Ranchers and roads do not mix with the needs of large wild animals.

The Greater Yellowstone Ecosystem Program is working to develop partnerships among public agencies, nongovernmental groups, and individuals to address ecosystem issues such as development and changes in fire patterns. Laura Hubbard, the Greater Yellowstone Program Manager for The Nature Conservancy, says the program could serve as a model for conservation efforts that develop partnerships among diverse groups to protect key natural areas.[1]

—The Editor

1. Series editor's personal communication with Laura Hubbard, September 13, 2004.

The Lone Rangers
by William Stolzenburg

The rumors began three years ago, of four-legged ghosts haunting the muscular flanks of the Absaroka Range east of Yellowstone National Park. The federal biologists tracking Wyoming's wolves eventually decided it was time to collar one of Carter Mountain's controversial new residents. Funny thing was, the wolf they trapped was already wearing one.

The wolf was identified as B58, a 4-year-old male. According to the logbook, B58 had been born to the Thunder Mountain Pack of central Idaho—330 air miles away.

Getting from there to here, B58 had scaled mountains, forded rivers, crossed plains and tiptoed solo through uncounted enemy lines of livestock fences, interstate highways, elk hunters and hostile wolf territories. He had more than spanned an immense checkerboard of federal parks and forests, private pastures, and human settlements known as the Greater Yellowstone Ecosystem. In doing so, he had circumscribed one of the great conservation challenges of the day.

B58 and his wolf kin of Greater Yellowstone are pivotal players in a grand ecological experiment, to expand what some see as a glorified zoo into something bigger and more befitting the land's widest-ranging wildlife. The zoo in question is the 2.2-million-acre Yellowstone National Park, housing the greatest assemblage of hoofed wildlife and big predators in the contiguous United States. The bigger-and-more-befitting something is the surrounding 25 million acres, where the megafauna naturally wander—lately through a tightening noose of humanity. How far would society have to go to let the elk run wild and the wolves be wolves? The journey of B58 provides one long and sobering yardstick.

A PLAN OF AUDACIOUS DIMENSIONS
In 1999 a team of independent scientists hired by the Greater Yellowstone Coalition and The Nature Conservancy began laying out a conservation plan of sweeping proportions. Its task, in

the simplest terms, was to preserve the biological diversity and integrity of an ecosystem the size of Tennessee. Centered by Yellowstone National Park, the Greater Yellowstone Ecosystem is a land of high volcanic plateau bounded by big mountains—the Absarokas, Beartooths, Wind Rivers and Tetons, with outlying ranges stretching east to the Bighorns of Wyoming and south to the Wasatch and Uinta of Utah. Within that rugged immensity lives a nearly complete suite of North American ungulates—among them, moose, deer, bison, pronghorn antelope and bighorn sheep—and carnivores, including black bear, cougar, wolverine and coyote. More prominently, it is one of the country's last strongholds for the grizzly bear; locus of the greatest concentration of elk in the world; and the recently established territory of some 30 packs of gray wolves.

The scientists' plan, which the Conservancy adopted, identified a network of sites across the ecosystem designed to safeguard Greater Yellowstone's rare species and full range of habitats, adding a special consideration for the large, space-gobbling, ecosystem-altering mammals whose needs entail a more radical concept of space.

When it came to the wide-ranging species, "we had to consider the concept of connectivity," says plan leader Reed Noss, now a professor of conservation biology at the University of Central Florida. That is to say, conserving Greater Yellowstone implied more than saving points A and B. Considering the big, predators and their prey, whose seasonal wanderings can cover hundreds of miles, the conservationist had to either connect the dots or shortcut the animals' life histories. A Yellowstone grizzly might cover 360 square miles in a year; a lonely teenage wolf like B58 may traverse states looking for a mate. For the wide rangers, Noss and his colleagues pointed out, there were places en route that once severed could never be replaced. And in Greater Yellowstone, there are many such places.

A WILDERNESS PARADOX

One of the wildest tracts in the Lower 48 [states], Greater Yellowstone is also one of the most besieged. From 1970 to

1997, the region's human population rose by 55 percent, with five of its 20 counties more than doubling. Residential development, with the allure of a world-class wilderness in the back yard, quadrupled during that period.

Collisions are inevitable. The famous menagerie of Yellowstone National Park makes short work of its protected confines, traversing the mountains and valleys that reach like arms and legs beyond the park and into the human gauntlet. Over the next 25 years, the capacity of those limbs to conduct wide rangers is due to be choked by a third. So predicts Carlos Carroll, an ecological modeler out of Orleans, California, and a co-author of the Greater Yellowstone plan. In his computer simulations, he sees a future of grizzlies wandering more often into hunting camps, wolves into cattle pastures, and elk into barbed wire and subdivisions. "Greater Yellowstone is at the threshold," Carroll says. "We now have the potential of protecting it as a functioning ecosystem, or losing it."

In late October, when the legendary cold descends on the high plateau of Yellowstone National Park, its borders begin spilling elk by the thousands. They migrate through the sur-rounding mountain passes to the lowlands, where the snowpack remains thin and the burdens of foraging lessen. Few of their migrations, forged over generations, have survived intact across the fragmenting landscape. One herd that still follows its ancient bearings heads southeast, through the southern peaks of the Absarokas to the Wind River Valley. Near the end of their journey, above the town of Dubois, Wyoming, the descending elk come upon the flash of new rooftops against the hillsides.

Once a simpler sort of cow town, Dubois has become a second-home community of the well-to-do, with magnificent log houses proliferating up the hillsides. What used to be free range for 6,500 elk is being parceled by new roads and ranchettes, with fences and barking dogs.

Around towns like Dubois, with Greater Yellowstone property at a premium and many ranches on the razor edge of profitability, developers circle hungrily. "You're a rancher looking across at your wife, you're 75 years old, you can't work anymore—what are you going to do?" asks Paula Hunker, associate state director for the Conservancy in Wyoming. "Your only hope is to sell it to somebody, and that's usually going to be a developer. That's what we're trying to stop." Beginning three years ago with the Winchester Ranch, the Conservancy has begun preserving, link by link, a chain of private lands and ranches running up and down the Wind River Valley through Dubois, trying to keep the elk lanes open.

And if it were merely a matter of smoothing the path for the Wind River elk, the battle for Dubois would be a less sticky affair. But lately in Greater Yellowstone, wherever the great herds of elk roam, big predators are not far behind.

Three years ago, as Debbie Robinett was walking with her dog to the barn, a pack of wolves swooped in and dragged the 110-pound Great Pyrenees into the darkness. At last count, the Pyrenees was one of seven dogs, two horses and dozens of calves that have been killed by wolves and grizzly bears over the past six years on the Diamond G, the ranch that Debbie and her husband, Jon, manage in the DuNoir Valley northwest of Dubois.

The Diamond G has become the poster child for carnivore–livestock conflicts in Greater Yellowstone. Jon Robinett says he's had upward of 30 grizzly bears removed from his property over the past decade. He's worked with biologists, moved his cattle away from grizzly dens and installed 8 miles of electric fence. And still he loses. "Last year I turned out 302 calves. Lost 30 of them," says Robinett, who prices them at $1,000 each. Five were confirmed wolf kills; others remain suspect. "It's just a futile battle," he says. "You can't expect ranchers to bear the whole cost of this. Ask any conservationist how much they give to wolves. If you'll contribute the same amount of money every year as I do, I'll never say another word."

Soon after the wolves were reintroduced to Yellowstone in 1995, in a nationally ballyhooed victory of the Endangered Species Act, Hank Fischer, then of the Defenders of Wildlife, extended the organization's predator compensation program to meet such challenges as the Robinetts'. Aiming to pay for and prevent losses of livestock to wolves and grizzlies, Defenders of Wildlife has since doled out more than a quarter million dollars to ranchers in the Rockies. According to Gina Shrader, Defenders' carnivore conservation coordinator, $21,691 of that has gone to the Diamond G.

At the Diamond G, Fischer sees more vindication than contradiction in the idea of wolves and livestock coexisting in Greater Yellowstone. "The Diamond G has had more problems than anywhere else in the Yellowstone ecosystem," says Fischer, now with the National Wildlife Federation. "But going out of business? I don't think so. I can't think of anyplace where wolves would have made the difference between profitability or not."

AN ECOSYSTEM DIVIDED

The dust-up in Dubois is of the sort arising wherever legal boundaries and local cultures run counter to Yellowstone's wide rangers. The skirmishes have even the conservationists wondering where to draw the lines.

"My grandfather was around when they were killing the last wolves," says Bob Budd, a fifth-generation Wyomingite, president of the Society for Range Management and project manager of the Conservancy's Red Canyon Ranch. "When you have a horse standing there with its hindquarters eaten off, it's a revolting thing. Now the public's asking the ranchers to do something that's detrimental to their well-being. We have to be very cautious when we make a choice. How does this affect my fellow human being?"

As for how human beings affect their competing predators, there is little question. It is a maxim of conservation biology that wherever big wild predators and people meet, the wild predators soon disappear. Grizzly bears once ranged from the Pacific Coast to the Great Plains; about 1,100 remain in a scattered handful of populations. A similar story can be told of the gray wolf, a coast-to-coast resident when the Europeans landed, exterminated in every state except Alaska and Minnesota by the 1960s. Gray wolves south of Canada now number about 3,800, in places to which they've recently been trucked or otherwise allowed by law to recolonize on their own.

And if recent history offers any lessons, even Yellowstone park is no sure place to keep your wolves.

Wildlife reserves around the world are losing species, and the wide-ranging carnivores are often the first to go. Lions in east Africa, snow leopards in Pakistan, tigers in Nepal—all have disappeared from reserves with boundaries too small and surroundings too hostile. Tanzania's Serengeti, with which the greatest of wildlife sanctuaries, including Yellowstone, are ultimately compared, no longer harbors its famed packs of African wild dogs, the continent's ecological counterpart to America's gray wolf. Yellowstone itself lost its wolves 50 years after the park was established.

Restoring Greater Yellowstone's wide-ranging nature transcends simple biology. "It's all about sociology and economic and perception," says Joni Ward, the Conservancy's lead scientist for the Greater Yellowstone plan. "If they get shot as soon as they cross the borders, then you don't have a functioning ecosystem. And if people don't want wolves and grizzlies, they're not going to be there."

The people's decision is pending. Three Wyoming counties on the edges of Greater Yellowstone last year declared gray wolves illegal. (The declarations—toothless, symbolic gestures at the time—have since been empowered with new bite by federal regulations that grant the states more latitude in managing their wolves.) Certain hunters and ranchers are more direct in their prescriptions. "Kill the son of a bitch the second he steps out of the park," says rancher Jack Turnell.

Turnell is past president of the Wyoming Stockgrowers Association. He has also been dubbed the Green Cowboy, the recipient of national conservation awards for his work in managing the amazing land he calls home, 17 miles west of Meeteetse, Wyoming. The Pitchfork Ranch spreads over 100,000 acres of grassy plains and conifer-forested hills, crowned on the western horizon by the jagged east wall of the Absarokas. Grizzlies wander down every spring to yank a calf or two out of Turnell's corral; a mountain lion has posed for pictures on his lawn. In 1981 a neighbor's dog brought home an animal that most biologists had written off as extinct, and for a while—until twin outbreaks of plague and distemper decimated the population—the Pitchfork was famous as the world's last wild home of the black-footed ferret.

The Pitchfork is as much wildlife reserve as cattle ranch. It is owned by longtime residents Turnell and his wife, Lili, and, more recently, two business partners from the Washington, D.C., area and the Conservancy. All parties want badly to keep the wildlife safe and the subdividers at bay in one of Greater

The Ecoregional Perspective

The Greater Yellowstone Ecosystem was first defined by biologists John and Frank Craighead as an area large enough to sustain Yellowstone's population of grizzly bears. Time and the evolution of conservation have determined that wasn't quite enough.

Over the decades, the philosophy of Greater Yellowstone conservation has grown bigger than the bear. The ecosystem's dimensions now include not only the grizzly but all the ecosystem's 1,600 or so native species, from wolf to whooping crane, Eureka mountainsnail to Graham's columbine.

The Greater Yellowstone plan that the Nature Conservancy has adopted, though a strategy known as ecoregional planning, suggests the scale at which modern conservation now operates. Ecological regions, or "ecoregions," are framed not by legal boundaries but by naturally delineated realms of climate and geology, fire and flood, and their corresponding cover of signature plants and animals. Examples in the Western Hemisphere include the sunlit, saguaro-studded Sonoran Desert and the coastal jungles of Brazil.

Within each region remain key tracts of nature collectively representing the whole, whose protection would conserve the region's native species. Conservancy scientists are now defining those portfolios of preserves, those networks of refuges that would conserve the greatest breadth of biodiversity for the long term.

—W. S.

Yellowstone's most majestic borderlands. Turnell, for his part, also has a livestock business to manage. He runs roughly 2,000 head, making cattle the second-most-common hoofed animal on the ranch. A herd of 800 elk lives year-round on the Pitchfork; another 2,500 elk journey here from Yellowstone National Park each fall, crossing 12,000-foot alpine passes to winter in the snow shadow of Carter Mountain. And as of three years ago, coinciding suspiciously with the disappearance of B58 from his natal mountains of central Idaho, there has also been a pack of wolves patrolling the backcountry of the Pitchfork.

Wolves are where the philosophies of Turnell and the wide-ranger champions diverge. "There's no use or reason for the wolf in this ecosystem," says Turnell. "Hell, wolves will start killing anything they see. They're not going to stop at the borders. They're going to keep chomping their way to Mexico, and you're going to see some of the biggest wildlife devastation you ever saw."

Turnell hammers his point: "The wolf is not an important part of the food chain and neither is the grizz'. Anybody says it is, is going to have to prove it to me."

That food chain is now under considerable scientific scrutiny. Since the wolves' return, the Greater Yellowstone Ecosystem's expanded web has become an ecologist's Mecca. The scientists' preliminary sketch looks something like this: Wolves—nearly 300 at last count—have saturated most of the available habitat in the park and immediate surroundings. They have been eating mainly elk, particularly calves and weak old cows, which the wolves are frequently forced to relinquish when a big grizzly comes swaggering. Grizzlies are guardedly flourishing, perhaps helped by the new windfall of wolf-killed elk meat. Elk are holding relatively stable; speculations about their inevitable extermination by wolves remain speculations.

There are signs that the recent splash of big predators is sending ecological ripples throughout the ecosystem. For the first time in more than a decade, a segment of the park's precarious herd of 200 pronghorn has begun to grow. The reason, suspects pronghorn expert John Byers of the University of Idaho, is that some of the pronghorn have begun to find refuge from their chief predator, the coyote, within the park's densest neighborhood of wolves—where the wolves' mortally hated little cousins fear to tread. Byers says, "It's likely wolves are going to be the single-most-important force to save the pronghorn of Yellowstone."

The top predators appear to have reached to the very roots of Yellowstone's ecology. With wolves back after a 70-year hiatus and emigrating grizzlies reclaiming old territories of their own, elk and moose have suddenly ceased lounging and browsing certain stream-side groves to stubble. Aspen have begun to sprout like never before in the past century. Beavers, eaters of aspen, have proliferated, establishing 77 colonies across the park. The beavers' pond-side groves harbor song-birds missing elsewhere. And so on.

Beyond their physical imprint, the returning carnivores have reinserted themselves into the psychology of Yellowstone wildlife. After vacationing from their ancient antagonists for generations, elk and moose are relearning their antipredator lessons. "We'd watch a wolf walk right up to elk or moose, who'd show no sign of worry," says Joel Berger, a wildlife biolo-gist with the Wildlife Conservation Society, who for more than a decade has been studying Greater Yellowstone's evolving predator-prey interactions. "Now they worry plenty. When the elk hear a wolf howl, they become highly vigilant. They run."

The Yellowstone studies have added weight to a growing body of evidence suggesting that big, wide-ranging predators matter very much; that Greater Yellowstone without its wide rangers is a tamer, more impoverished place; that the park without its surroundings remains a shadow of its wildest potential.

Yet there remain those who declare the era of the free rangers past, the ideal of Eden dead. "Nature today is not as it was in 1850," says Turnell. "When I was born, there were 2 billion people. Now there's 6, and there's gonna be twice that many. How are we going to accommodate that growth? Truth is, Yellowstone National Park is a zoo. What do you do? Kill all the people? Or do you accommodate the zoo? I'm for the zoo."

At last notice, the young Greybull Pack of wolf B58 was still roaming the upper reaches of the Pitchfork, but now beneath the cloud of suspicion. Last spring, wolves apparently killed two cattle in the herd belonging to Turnell's neighbor. A federal trapper was given orders to determine the guilty party. "We're not going to go looking for them," said wolf biologist Mike Jimenez of the U.S. Fish and Wildlife Service. "But if they cause problems again, it will be the third time. If it's on private property, we will do control."

In the euphemistic vernacular of organized predator management, *control* typically translates to *kill*. For B58 and Greater Yellowstone, *control* might also mean the symbolic end of a long, unfinished journey home.

How Did the Writings of Rachel Carson Make *Conservation* a Household Word?

There are a handful of individuals who can be counted among those responsible for introducing the ideas that shaped the modern-day environmental movement in the United States. Ralph Waldo Emerson, Henry Thoreau, John Muir, and Theodore Roosevelt provided the initial ideas that shaped American thoughts on the importance of conservation. In the 1960s, a woman biologist who had devoted her entire life to studying and writing about nature, wrote a book that sparked the imagination of the American public. Her name was Rachel Carson, and she published the controversial *Silent Spring* in 1962. It has been reprinted in nearly 20 languages. The following are excerpts from the book.

The title of Carson's book, *Silent Spring*, refers to the quiet mornings that have become common in the years since innumerable birds have been killed by the pesticides sprayed on the fish, insects, or rodents they eat. The book served as a warning and a plea to Americans to stop spreading poisons on the land. In beautiful prose, Carson presented the idea that we are all connected—what poisons one, can poison all.

Carson's life is the story of a passionate woman dedicated to a cause we are still fighting today: honoring the connection among all living things and creating a healthy environment in which to live. Her dedication to *Silent Spring* read: "To Albert Schweitzer, who said, 'Man has lost the capacity to foresee and to forestall. He will end by destroying the earth.'"

But more than just warnings, her writing made the beauty and wonder of nature accessible to her readers. More than 40 years after *Silent Spring* was published, her words are still inspiring those who work toward ensuring a cleaner world.

—The Editor

Silent Spring
by Rachel Carson

"THE OBLIGATION TO ENDURE"

THE HISTORY OF LIFE on earth has been a history of interaction between living things and their surroundings. To a large extent, the physical form and the habits of the earth's vegetation and its animal life have been molded by the environment. Considering the whole span of earthly time, the opposite effect, in which life actually modifies its surroundings, has been relatively slight. Only within the moment of time represented by the present century has one species—man—acquired significant power to alter the nature of his world.

During the past quarter century this power has not only increased to one of disturbing magnitude but it has changed in character. The most alarming of all man's assaults upon the environment is the contamination of air, earth, rivers, and sea with dangerous and even lethal materials. This pollution is for the most part irrecoverable; the chain of evil it initiates not only in the world that must support life but in living tissues is for the most part irreversible. In this now universal contamination of the environment, chemicals are the sinister and little-recognized partners of radiation in changing the very nature of the world—the very nature of its life. Strontium 90, released through nuclear explosions into the air, comes to earth in rain or drifts down as fallout, lodges in soil, enters into the grass or corn or wheat grown there, and in time takes up its abode in the bones of a human being, there to remain until his death. Similarly, chemicals sprayed on croplands or forests or gardens lie long in soil, entering into living organisms, passing from one to another in a chain of poisoning and death. Or they pass mysteriously by underground streams until they emerge and, through the alchemy of air and sunlight, combine into new forms that kill vegetation, sicken cattle, and work unknown harm on those who drink from once pure wells. As Albert Schweitzer has said, "Man can hardly even recognize the devils of his own creation."

It took hundreds of millions of years to produce the life that now inhabits the earth—eons of time in which that developing and evolving and diversifying life reached a state of adjustment and balance with its surroundings. The environment, rigorously shaping and directing the life it supported, contained elements that were hostile as well as supporting. Certain rocks gave out dangerous radiation; even within the light of the sun, from which all life draws its energy, there were short-wave radiations with power to injure. Given time—time not in years but in millennia—life adjusts, and a balance has been reached. For time is the essential ingredient; but in the modern world there is no time.

The rapidity of change and the speed with which new situations are created follow the impetuous and heedless pace of man rather than the deliberate pace of nature. Radiation is no longer merely the background radiation of rocks, the bombardment of cosmic rays, the ultraviolet of the sun that have existed before there was any life on earth; radiation is now the unnatural creation of man's tampering with the atom. The chemicals to which life is asked to make its adjustment are no longer merely the calcium and silica and copper and all the rest of the minerals washed out of the rocks and carried in rivers to the sea; they are the synthetic creations of man's inventive mind, brewed in his laboratories, and having no counterparts in nature.

To adjust to these chemicals would require time on the scale that is nature's; it would require not merely the years of a man's life but the life of generations. And even this, were it by some miracle possible, would be futile, for the new chemicals come from our laboratories in an endless stream; almost five hundred annually find their way into actual use in the United States alone. The figure is staggering and its implications are not easily grasped—500 new chemicals to which the bodies of men and animals are required somehow to adapt each year, chemicals totally outside the limits of biologic experience.

Among them are many that are used in man's war against nature. Since the mid-1940s over 500 basic chemicals have been created for use in killing insects, weeds, rodents, and other organisms described in the modern vernacular as "pests"; and they are sold under several thousand different brand names.

These sprays, dusts, and aerosols are now applied almost universally to farms, gardens, forests, and homes—nonselective chemicals that have the power to kill every insect, the "good" and the "bad," to still the song of birds and the leaping of fish in the streams, to coat the leaves with a deadly film, and to linger on in soil—all this though the intended target may be only a few weeds or insects. Can anyone believe it is possible to lay down such a barrage of poisons on the surface of the earth without making it unfit for all life? They should not be called "insecticides," but "biocides."

The whole process of spraying seems caught up in an endless spiral. Since DDT was released for civilian use, a process escalation has been going on in which ever more toxic materials must be found. This has happened because insects, in a triumphant vindication of Darwin's principle of the survival of the fittest, have evolved super races immune to the particular insecticide used, hence a deadlier one has always to be developed—and then a deadlier one than that. It has happened also because, for reasons to be described later, destructive insects often undergo a "flareback," or resurgence, after spraying, in numbers greater than before. Thus the chemical war is never won, and all life is caught in its violent crossfire.

Along with the possibility of the extinction of mankind by nuclear war, the central problem of our age has therefore become the contamination of man's total environment with such substances of incredible potential for harm—substances that accumulate in the tissues of plants and animals and even penetrate the germ cells to shatter or alter the very material of heredity upon which the shape of the future depends. All this is not to say there is no insect problem and no need of control. I am saying, rather, that control must be geared to realities, not to mythical situations, and that the methods employed must be such that they do not destroy us along with the insects. . . .

It is not my contention that chemical insecticides must never be used. I do contend that we have put poisonous and biologically potent chemicals indiscriminately into the hands of persons largely or wholly ignorant of their potentials for harm. We have subjected enormous numbers of people to contact with these poisons, without their consent and often without their knowledge. If the Bill of Rights contains no guarantee that a citizen shall be secure against lethal poisons distributed either by private individuals or by public officials, it is surely only because our forefathers, despite their considerable wisdom and foresight, could conceive of no such problem.

I contend, furthermore, that we have allowed these chemicals to be used with little or no advance investigation of their effect on soil, water, wildlife, and man himself. Future generations are unlikely to condone our lack of prudent concern for the integrity of the natural world that supports all life.

There is still very limited awareness of the nature of the threat. This is an era of specialists, each of whom sees his own problem and is unaware of or intolerant of the larger frame into which it fits. It is also an era dominated by industry, in which the right to make a dollar at whatever cost is seldom challenged. When the public protests, confronted with some obvious evidence of damaging results of pesticide applications, it is fed little tranquilizing pills of half truth. We urgently need an end to these false assurances, to the sugar coating of unpalatable facts. It is the public that is being asked to assume the risks that the insect controllers calculate. The public must decide whether it wishes to continue on the present road, and it can do so only when in full possession of the facts. In the words of Jean Rostand, "The obligation to endure gives us the right to know."

"THE OTHER ROAD"

We stand now where two roads diverge. But unlike the roads in Robert Frost's familiar poem, they are not equally fair. The road we have long been traveling is deceptively easy, a smooth super-highway on which we progress with great speed, but at its end lies disaster. The other fork of the road—the one "less traveled by"—offers our last, our only chance to reach a destination that assures the preservation of our earth.

The choice, after all, is ours to make. If, having endured much, we have at last asserted our "right to know," and if, knowing, we have concluded that we are being asked to take senseless and frightening risks, then we should no longer accept the counsel of those who tell us that we must fill our world with poisonous chemicals; we should look about and see what other course is open to us.

A truly extraordinary variety of alternatives to the chemical control of insects is available. Some are already in use and have achieved brilliant success. Others are in the stage of laboratory testing. Still others are little more than ideas in the minds of imaginative scientists, waiting for the opportunity to put them to the test. All have this in common: they are *biological* solutions, based on understanding of the living organisms they seek to control, and of the whole fabric of life to which these organisms belong. Specialists representing various areas of the vast field of biology are contributing—entomologists, pathologists, geneticists, physiologists, biochemists, ecologists—all pouring their knowledge and their creative inspirations into the formation of a new science of biotic controls.

Through all these new, imaginative, and creative approaches to the problem of sharing our earth with other creatures there runs a constant theme, the awareness that we are dealing with life—with living populations and all their pressures and counterpressures, their surges and recessions. Only by taking account of such life forces and by cautiously seeking to guide them into channels favorable to ourselves can we hope to achieve a reasonable accommodation between the insect hordes and ourselves.

The current vogue for poisons has failed utterly to take into account these most fundamental considerations. As crude a weapon as the cave man's club, the chemical barrage has been hurled against the fabric of life—a fabric on the one hand delicate and destructible, on the other miraculously tough and resilient, and capable of striking back in unexpected ways. These extraordinary capacities of life have been ignored by the practitioners of chemical control who have brought to their task no "high-minded orientation," no humility before the vast forces with which they tamper.

The "control of nature" is a phrase conceived in arrogance, born of the Neanderthal age of biology and philosophy, when it was supposed that nature exists for the convenience of man. The concepts and practices of applied entomology for the most part date from that Stone Age of science. It is our alarming misfortune that so primitive a science has armed itself with the most modern and terrible weapons, and that in turning them against the insects it has also turned them against the earth.

Why Are Volunteers out Looking for Frogs and Salamanders Every Spring?

Forest pools may be small and may disappear in the heat of every summer, but to some people in Maine, as the following article shows, they are VIPs—Very Important Pools. VIPs are vernal pools, the pools that form in the forest after spring rains and provide safe breeding spots for amphibians—frogs, toads, and salamanders. A volunteer monitoring program, the Maine VIP program, was started in 1999 and has grown into a dedicated group of people who have collected more vernal pool data than exists in any other state.

Amphibians play an important role in forest ecosystems. Biologist Michael Klemens calls them the "energy cells of this forest ecosystem" because of their role in cycling nutrients and, in turn, providing food for many larger animals.[1] When vernal pools are destroyed by development or the forests around them are cut down, amphibian populations suffer. Loss of habitat is just one reason for the declining amphibian populations. The other reasons are varied: from habitat destruction to global warming to pesticides to diseases and parasites.[2] A declining amphibian population is a conservation issue because it is a warning signal of problems in the overall health of our environment.[3]

Aram Calhoun, who spearheaded the Maine VIP program, worked with Michael Clemens of the Wildlife Conservation Society to develop a manual of Best Management Practices for protecting vernal pools. These measures are now being incorporated into many municipal plans and are being considered for use in other states. Calhoun credits the devoted volunteer force—made up of Maine retirees, students, biologists, foresters, and entire class-rooms of students—with bringing the importance of vernal pools into the public eye. Public awareness of the ecological importance of vernal pools helps get better management practices adopted.

The Maine VIP program serves as an example of how people are working on many different levels to protect parts of the ecosystem. And when one part is protected, the whole system benefits.

—The Editor

145

1. Stutz, Bruce. "Thinking Like a Salamander." *OnEarth*. Natural Resources Defense Council, Summer 2004.

2. Blaustein, Michael R. "Vanishing Amphibians." *Defenders*, Summer 2001.

3. Semlitsch, Raymond D. *Amphibian Conservation*. Washington, D.C.: Smithsonian Books, 2002, p. 2.

The Frog Squad
by Christine Parrish

Every spring cadres of volunteers fan out across the state to study all the activity in the woodland puddles known as vernal pools. Spearheading the effort is one very determined woman with a pair of hip boots and a passion for frogs.

As a small ten-year-old, Aram Calhoun patrolled the red maple swamps of her rural Rhode Island neighborhood in search of kids who caught bullfrogs and squashed them on the road.

When she found them, she jumped them.

She took down her neighbor, Billy Joe, and made him release his frogs. Then she won him over to her side. Together, they patrolled the swamp, jumping the bullfrog bullies and winning them over. Soon, a whole platoon of kids were catching frogs and then happily letting them go.

Thirty years later, Aram Calhoun's approach has not changed. As a respected wetlands ecologist with a dual position at the Maine Audubon Society and the University of Maine, she is still jumping into swamps and winning people over to her side.

Only this time, she is not just out to protect frogs; she is out to protect their homes—wicked big puddles in the woods known as vernal pools. Once thought of as low areas in the forests that collected rainwater and bred mosquitoes, scientists have found vernal pools to be a rich biological soup that support a wide array of forest wildlife from early spring when the pools form to late summer when they dry up.

They do not, however, support fish. And it is this that makes them unique. Created by rainwater and snowmelt, vernal pools have no inlet or outlet to let fish in. Even if they did get in, low dissolved oxygen levels would not allow them to survive for long. But lack of oxygen is no handicap for four wildlife species that can only succeed in raising offspring in a fishless environment: the fingernail-sized fairy shrimp; the spotted salamander, whose yellow polka-dot markings are as vivid as a rain slicker; the blue-spotted salamander, which is speckled like a blue enamelware pot; and the wood frog, a little brown frog with a black robber's mask.

While these four species can produce young that survive in a nursery pool that starts out rimmed with ice and gets warmer and more stagnant before drying up in late summer, the youngsters have no defense against predatory fish. When wood frogs and spotted salamanders inadvertently lay eggs in ponds or beaver flowages, fish gobble up the eggs as quickly as caviar disappears at a cocktail party. The result: no young frogs or salamanders survive.

Even with the absence of fish, vernal pools are veritable buffet tables during early spring when there is not much else for woodland wildlife to eat. Everything from birds to bears loves those eggs. In theory, if every salamander and wood frog egg survived to grow up and hop and slither across the forest floor, we would be chest deep in amphibians. In fact, as a food source, vernal pool amphibians and their eggs are naturally so abundant that wetlands ecologists think vernal pools are a key thread in the Maine forest food web.

Ten years ago little was known, and few cared, about these small forested wetlands that are often no larger than a living room. But change came fast to the forests of Maine. While the state remains over 90 percent forested, the forest is breaking up in the southern half of the state where rapid-fire residential development has grown 30 percent over the last ten years. In the northern part of the state, huge blocks of timberland changed hands almost overnight in the mid-nineties, leaving its future management uncertain. Larger wetlands had been studied extensively and were protected by state and federal laws, but few scientists were investigating wetlands smaller than a third of an acre. Those who did study vernal pools found them to be incredibly productive ecosystems that were falling through the regulatory gaps. By the mid-nineties there was a growing sense that important wildlife habitat was being lost before anyone knew how important it really was.

That is when Aram Calhoun pulled up her hip boots and jumped right in.

In 1996, Calhoun, then finishing her doctorate at the University of Maine, put her head together with Sally Stockwell, director of conservation at Maine Audubon Society, and applied for a grant from the Switzer Foundation to fund field research on vernal pools in York County. This work led to more rounds of fund-raising, and the beginning of the Maine Audubon's Very Important Pool (VIP) project to recruit and train volunteers to gather physical data about the pools (including pool size, temperature, and water depth) and to determine the presence of vernal pool species.

On a shoestring budget, Calhoun trained a small squad of volunteers to collect data from a handful of pools in the spring of 1999. By 2002, she commanded an army of volunteers to make a three-year commitment to take up clipboards, don waders, and head into the woods during blackfly season to count wood frog and spotted salamander eggs in vernal pools across the state. By the end of the 2003 field season, Calhoun's VIP volunteers will have collected more data on more vernal pools than exists anywhere else in the world.

In a shady woodland within Orono city limits, Calhoun watches from the shore as veteran VIP volunteer John Maddaus cautiously wades into a thigh-deep pool in search of blue-spotted salamander eggs.

Aram Calhoun affectionately named the pool Lost Pond because the path to it starts at a city street and leads through birch and pine trees to the crest of a hill where the woods suddenly open up to reveal the vernal pool shimmering in the sunlight.

"I love it. It's like a little fairyland hidden in the woods," says Calhoun. "It's fantastic, isn't it?"

No argument there. Wood frogs mated at the pool in April and their eggs have already hatched into small black tadpoles that dart about in the tea-brown water. Flycatchers swoop above the water, grabbing mosquitoes to feed their nestlings, and a pair of wood ducks hide behind shrubs sprouting up in the middle of the pool before flying off. A host of other wildlife, including raccoons, dragonflies, gray tree frogs, and bullfrogs also come to the pool to feed, breed, or laze about on a regular basis.

"And it's so ephemeral," Calhoun adds. By September, all that will be left is a small grassy meadow at the top of the. hill with a few sedges to reveal to the trained eye that it really is a wetland.

"Where did you find the blue-spotted eggs last time you were here, John? In shallow water?" Calhoun asks. She has been relentlessly questioning Maddaus about his data-collection techniques since arriving at the pool ten minutes earlier. Her tone suggests Maddaus is a scientific colleague or one of her corps of graduate students rather than a volunteer with no formal scientific training. And she wants to know the answers. Calhoun relies on VIP volunteers to stimulate her thinking on what information gaps exist that she might address through future research.

"In less than a foot of water," Maddaus replies. "On the sunnier end of the pool."

Maddaus knows the blue-spotted eggs are here—he has found them every year for the past four years—but they are hard to see in the dark water. Like the yellow-spotted salamanders, the blue-spotted salamanders are land dwellers; they do not live in vernal pools, but in the surrounding shady forest where they spend 95 percent of their lives. By day, they hide underground in abandoned mole holes. By night, they forage for food on the forest floor. For a short time every spring they migrate en masse to mate in the same vernal pool where they themselves hatched.

Of the four vernal pool species, the presence of the blue-spotted salamander is the most difficult to detect. They do not breed in every pool, and their translucent eggs are remarkably hard to see beneath the surface of the water. Finding their eggs is something like winning the prize at the county fair; it takes luck and perseverance and the odds are long. Maddaus did not see any eggs in the water during his first salamander egg count of the year until he gently lifted submerged twigs towards the water surface.

"There were thousands upon thousands of blue-spotted eggs in this pool," says Maddaus. "Masses of eggs dripped from the branches like jeweled necklaces. But you couldn't see them from the surface."

They have since hatched out to small tadpole-like larva adept at hiding on the bottom of the pool. Not one is in sight.

"Do the blue spotted hatch before the yellow spotted in this pool?" Calhoun asks. Research on vernal pools is still new enough that there are a lot of unanswered questions. No one is sure, for instance, exactly how rare the blue-spotted salamander is in the state of Maine.

Maddaus replies that they do.

Suddenly, Calhoun's dispassionate inquiry drops like a stone.

"Oh, John. Will you look at that? Just look at that," Calhoun says, pointing into the water and almost jumping in without her rubber boots on. She has spotted log cabin caddisfly larvae, which can be recognized by the tube of sticks they build around themselves, log cabin–style, as protection against predators. Hundreds of the inch-long larvae cling to a mass of spotted salamander eggs, looking like a miniature log cabin house kit that exploded and scattered haphazardly across a blob of clear Jell-O.

"What are they eating?" Calhoun asks. "Do you know? Are they just grazing the algae on the egg surface or are they sucking out the eggs?"

Calhoun, the respected scientist, would never interfere to save the salamander eggs. She knows better than most that an essential part of the function of those eggs in the ecological scheme of things is to provide food for others. Still, the woman who sometimes wears socks with little frogs printed on them when speaking at public events appears to be sorely tempted to jump.

Phillip deMaynadier, a wildlife biologist who is the point person for vernal pools at the Maine Department of Inland Fisheries and Wildlife, notes that it is Calhoun's passion for vernal pool frogs and salamanders combined with her scientific integrity that makes the difference. "Aram raised the profile of vernal pools across the state, both by her volunteer program and through public workshops," he explains. "If you mentioned vernal pools ten years ago, the term drew a blank stare."

Now, says deMaynadier, they are talked about at town meetings and in forest industry boardrooms.

That talk, much to Calhoun's gratification, has finally turned into on-the-ground action. Calhoun and deMaynadier developed a set of voluntary guidelines to protect vernal pools and adjacent forest habitat during logging operations. The Habitat Management Guidelines for Harvesting Timber around Vernal Pools, which were published in the summer of 2002, recommend a circular protection zone shaped like a dartboard, with the pool itself as the bull's eye. This leaves the pool undisturbed by skidders and other logging equipment, keeps a well-shaded forest within a hundred feet of the pool where many young salamanders and wood frogs linger after leaving the water, and minimizes logging activity within four hundred feet of the pool where adult salamanders live year-round.

Calhoun and deMaynadier crafted the first guidelines in 1998, but the forestry community balked at their severity. After soliciting input from industry representatives, the Maine Forest Service, the Maine Audubon Society, the University of Maine, and others, Calhoun and deMaynadier came up with a set of guidelines realistic enough to be implemented. In an understated diplomatic coup, they won over the forest management community and retained support from environmental groups. The Maine Forest Service sanctioned the guidelines and, today, industry leaders like International Paper voluntarily put them into practice on the ground.

"It took *years* to come up with a workable compromise and the forestry guidelines aren't perfect," admits Calhoun. "But they are based on the best science available today." Most importantly, she adds, the guidelines are being used.

They are, in fact, the first detailed habitat management guidelines for vernal pools in the country and states from as far away as Michigan and as close as Pennsylvania are interested in adapting them for use at home.

Still, Calhoun considers vernal pool conservation in highly developed areas much more pressing. "Even clear-cuts grow back," she says. Parking lots and housing developments, she points out, are forever.

Residential and commercial development pressures throughout New England led Calhoun to work with Michael Clemons of the Wildlife Conservation Society in New York state to create step-by-step guidelines to help towns and cities include vernal pool conservation in their overall planning process. Published last year, the Best Development Practices, or BDPs, have been embraced by the city of Falmouth.

Carson, Rachel. *Silent Spring*. Boston: Houghton Mifflin Company, 1987.

Ellis, Richard. *The Empty Ocean*. Washington, D.C.: Island Press, 2003.

Hinrichsen, Don. "A Human Thirst." *World Watch Institute Magazine*. January–February 2003.

Levin, Ted. "Reviving a River of Grass." *Audubon*. July–August 2001. Available online at *http://magazine.audubon.org/features0107/ecology/ecology0107.html*.

Parrish, Christine. "The Frog Squad." *Down East*. May 2003.

Pew Oceans Commission. *America's Living Oceans: Charting a Course for Sea Change*. 2003. Available online at *http://www.pewoceans.org/oceans/downloads/oceans_report.pdf*.

Postel, Sandra, and Brian Richter. *Rivers for Life*. Washington, D.C.: Island Press, 2003.

Shabecoff, Philip. "The Story Until Now." *Earth Rising*. Washington, D.C.: Island Press, 2003.

Stolzenburg, William. "The Lone Rangers." *The Nature Conservancy*. Fall 2003.

Summerhays, Soames. "Rescuing Reefs in Hot Water." *The Nature Conservancy*. Summer 2002.

Tolme, Paul. "Made in the Shade." *Audubon*. August 2004. Available online at *http://magazine.audubon.org/features0408/mexico.html*.

Wilson, E. O. *The Future of Life*. New York: Alfred A. Knopf, 2002.

FURTHER READING

Carson, Rachel. *Silent Spring.* Boston: Houghton Mifflin Company, 1987.

Dowie, Mark. *Losing Ground: American Environmentalism at the Close of the Twentieth Century.* Cambridge, MA: MIT Press, 1995.

Ellis, Richard. *The Empty Ocean.* Washington, D.C.: Island Press, 2003.

Postel, Sandra, and Brian Richter. *Rivers for Life.* Washington, D.C.: Island Press, 2003.

Turco, Richard P. *Earth Under Siege: From Air Pollution to Global Change.* New York: Oxford University Press, 2002.

Wilson, E. O., ed. *Biodiversity.* Washington, D.C.: National Academies Press, 1988.

———. *Diversity of Life.* Cambridge, MA: Harvard University Press, 1992.

WEBSITES

Natural Resources Defense Council
http://www.nrdc.org/

Pew Oceans Commission
http://www.pewoceans.org/oceans/downloads/oceans_report.pdf

U.S. Environmental Protection Agency
http://www.epa.gov/

Acidophiles, 6
Agriculture Organization of the United Nations (FAO), 72, 108
Agriculture, U.S. Department of, 23
Albatrosses, 74
Alien invaders, freshwater, 111
Alkaliphiles, 6
Alligators, Chinese, 110
American Heart Association, x
American Scientist (magazine), 79
America's Living Ocean: Charting a Course for Sea Change (Pew), 48
Amphibians, 18, 107, 147, 148–150
Ants, 16
Applebaum, Stuart, 119
Aquaculture, 51, 66, 81–84, 111
Aral Sea, 103, 110–112
Archaea, 5
Arctic National Wildlife Refuge, xxii
Army Corps of Engineers, U.S., 119–121
Aspirin, ix
Audubon (magazine), ix, x
Audubon Society, xxii, 38

Bacteria, 5
Bald eagle, xii–xiii
Barophiles, 6
Biodiversity (Wilson), viii, xxiii
Biodiversity
 overview, 2–3
 biosphere as Gaia, 12
 classification of species, 13–15
 defined, xiv, 2
 discovery of new species and, 17–20

ecosystem cycles, 11–12
freshwater flows and, 90
habitat destruction and, 106–107
human as rain forest, 20–21
levels of, 11
molecular revolution and, 15–16
Biologists, classification, 12
Biomass pyramid, 15
Bird Friendly program (Smithsonian), 42
Birds, 19–20, 107, 111
Blue revolution, 103, 113–14
Brazil, 40
Browner, Carol, x
Budd, Bob, 130
Bush, George H. W., 31
Bycatch, 65, 71–72, 82

Calhoun, Aram, 145–152
Callisto, 8–9
Cannery Row (Steinbeck), 68
Capture, unintentional, 71
Carnivore-livestock conflicts (Yellowstone), 129–130
Carroll, Carlos, 128
Carson, Rachel, xxi, 23, 28, 138
Carter, Jimmy, xxii
Causey, Billy, 60, 62
CERP (Comprehensive Everglades Restoration Plan), 116–119
Chad, Lake, 112–113
Challenger Deep (Mariana Trench), 6
China, water shortage and, 108–110
Chroococcidiopsis, 7

CITES (Convention on International Trade in Endangered Species), xiii, xxiv
Clean Air Act of 1970, ix–x, 29
Clean Water Act of 1972 (CWA), 93–94, 99
Coal, burning of, xv
Coastal Zone Management Act, 52
Coffee Belt, 41
Coffee, shade-grown. *See* Shade-coffee farms
Coles, Steve, 59
Commoner, Barry, 28
Comprehensive Everglades Restoration Plan (CERP), 116–119
Conservation, in U.S., xx–xxiii
Conservation International on climate change, xxiii–xxiv
Consilience (Wilson), 100
Constitution, U.S., 92, 93
Convention on International Trade in Endangered Species (CITES), xiii, xxiv
Coral bleaching, 57
Coral Reef Task Force, U.S., 56
Coral reefs
 overview, 55
 Bali symposium presentation, 62
 breakthrough on saving, 61–62
 coral bleaching, 58–59
 evolutionary success of, 59–60
 legislation to protect, 64
 in Palau, Micronesia, 56–57
 upwellings and, 61–62

INDEX

Crabs, horseshoe, 53
Craighead, John and
    Frank, 132
Cuyahoga River fire, xxi
CWA (Clean Water Act
    of 1972), 92, 93–94,
    99
Cyanobacteria, 7

Daniel, Hawhorne, 68
Davis, Gary, 69
DDT, banning of,
    xii–xiii, 51
Debt-for-Nature programs,
    xxiv
Defenders of Wildlife, 26,
    129–130
Deinococcus radiodurans,
    6–7
DeMaynadier, Phillip,
    151
Diamond-G Ranch
    (Yellowstone),
    129–130
Dietsch, Thomas, 41
"Diminishing Returns"
    (*National Geographic*),
    69
The Diversity of Life
    (Wilson), xiv
DNA sequences, 5
Dolphins, 76–77,
    109–110
Drift nets, 75–78
Dubois, W. Y., 128–129
Ducks Unlimited, 26
Dunkin' Donuts, 44

Earle, Sylvia, 72
Earth Day, 28
Earth Rising (Shabecoff),
    22
Earthtrust, 76
Ecosystem, defined, 53
EEZ (Exclusive Economic
    Zone), 48
Ehrlich, Paul, 28
El Niños, 57, 68

El Triunfo Biosphere
    Reserve, 44
Eldredge, Niles, ix, xiii
Ellis, Gerry, xiii
Ellis, Richard, 65
Emerson, Ralph Waldo,
    22, 138
The Empty Ocean (Ellis),
    65
Endangered Species Act
    of 1973, 70, 92, 129
Environmental Action,
    29
Environmental Defense
    Fund, 29
ENVIRONMENTAL ISSUES
    series
    Air Quality, xvi
    Climate Change,
        xvi
    Conservation,
        xvii–xviii
    Environmental Policy,
        xviii–xix
    Water Pollution,
        xix–xx
    Wildlife Protection,
        xx
Environmental movement
    overview, 22–23
    end of golden age,
        30–31
    first wave of, 23–26
    fourth wave of, 35
    industrial growth and,
        26–27
    new challenges to,
        33–35
    organizations founded,
        26
    postwar period, 27
    second wave, 27–30
    third wave of, 31–33
EPA (U.S. Environmental
    Protection Agency), 23,
    28
Escherichia coli, 6
Estes, James, 80

Ethics
    land, xxiv, 48
    water, 54, 99–102
Eukarya, 5
Europa, 8–9
Everglades National Park
    (Florida)
    overview, viii, 116–117
    Army Corps of
        Engineers and,
        116–119, 123
    decline of natural
        resources in, 116–118
    decline of species in,
        121
    designations of, 116
    ecological extremes of,
        120
    future dreams for,
        123–124
    restoration plan for
        (CERP), 116–119
    water politics and,
        121–123
Exclusive Economic
    Zone (EEZ), 48
"Extinction Risk in the
    Sea" (Roberts and
    Hawkins), 70
Extremophiles, 4–5
*Eye of the Albatross:
    Visions of Hope and
    Survival* (Safina),
    74–75

Falkenmark, Malin,
    113
FAO (Agriculture
    Organization of the
    United Nations),
    72, 108
Faraday, Michael, 16
Federal authorities for
    protecting U.S. rivers,
    94–95
Federal Energy Regula-
    tory Commission
    (FERC), 99

Federal Water Pollution Control Act, 29
FERC (Federal Energy Regulatory Commission), 99
A Fierce Green Fire (Shabecoff), 22
Finca Irlanda coffee farm, 38
Fischer, Hank, 129, 130
Fish and Wildlife Service, U.S., 123, 135
Fish farming. *See* Aquaculture
Fisheries, decline of, 49–50, 65–68
Fishing, longline, 73
Florida Everglades. *See* Everglades National Park
Florida Keys, 51
Florida Keys National Marine Sanctuary, 62
Food chain, fishing down the (Pauley), 79–80
Ford, William, xi
Forestry, U.S. Department of, 22
Freshwater resources overview, 103–104
    alien invaders and, 111
    blue revolution and, 113–114
    China and, 108–110
    competition for, 104–105, 108
    Lake Chad and, 112–113
    plant life and, 111
    pollution threats to, 108
    withdrawals from, 105–106
Friends of the Earth, 29

The Future of Life (Wilson), 2–3

Gaia, 11–12
Gainghan Plain (China), 109
Getches, David, 91
Gibbs, Lois Marie, xxii, 30
Gill nets, 75
Global Water Policy Project (Amherst, MA), 88, 105
Glynn, Peter, 59
Golden age of environmentalism, 30
Gorsuch, Anne (Burford), 31
Great Barrier Reef Marine Park (Australia), 60, 62
Great Depression, 27
Great Lakes water, 101–102
Greater Yellowstone Coalition, 126
Greater Yellowstone Ecosystem Program, 125, 127, 132
Greenhouse gases (GHG), xvi–xvii
Greenpeace, 29, 76
Greenwire (magazine), 22

Haaker, Peter, 69
Habitat destruction, 106–107
Habitat Management Guidelines for Harvesting Timber around Vernal Pools, 151
Hardin, Garrett, 28
Harpoons, 73
Hatziolos, Marea, 62–63
Hawkins, Julie, 70

Hays, Samuel P., 25
Health, human, ix–x, 29
Heisler, Lorraine, 122, 123
Hinrichsen, Don, 103–104
Horseshoe crabs, 53
Hubbard, Laura, 125
Human health, viii, ix–x, 29
A Human Thirst (Hinrichsen), 103–104
Hunker, Paula, 128–129
Huxley, Thomas, 67–68
Hyperthermophiles, 5–6

IJC (International Joint Commission), 101–102
IMF (International Monetary Fund), xxiv
Impacts, national, ix
Important Bird Areas, 38
Index Kewensis, 17
The Inexhaustible Sea (Hawthorne and Minot), 68
Instream flow water rights, 98
International Biosphere Reserve (Everglades), 116
International Coral Reef Symposium (9th), 62
International Fisheries Exhibition (London), 67
International Joint Commission (IJC), 101–102
International Whaling Commission (IWC), xxiii, 65
Io, 8–9
Irrigation from rivers, 89
IWC (International Whaling Commission), xxiii, 65

Izaak Walton League of America, 26

Jefferson County v. *Washington Department of Ecology*, 99
Jefferson, Thomas, 90
Jimenez, Mike, 135
Jupiter, 8–9

Kissimmee River (Florida), 116, 120
Klemens, Michael, 145
Komodo National Park (Indonesia), 61
Krchnak, Karin, 105, 113
Kyoto Protocol, x–xi, xxiv

LaBudde, Sam, 76
Lake Chad, 112–113
Lake Okeechobee (Florida), 51
Lake Vostok (Antarctica), 9
Land ethic, xxiv, 48
League of Conservation Voters in 1970, 30
Leopold, Aldo, xxi, xxiv, 28
Linnaean system of classification, 12–15
Longline fishing, 73
Lost Pond, 148
Love Canal case, 30
Lovelock, James E., 11–12

Maddaus, John, 148–149
Maine Audubon Society, 146, 151
Maine Audubon's Very Important Pool project (VIP), 148
Maine Department of Inland Fisheries and Wildlife, 151

Maine Forest Service, 151
Maine, University of, 151
Malakoff, David, x
Mammals, new, 18
Mandela, Nelson, 89
Mariana Trench, 6
Mars, 8–9
Marsh, George Perkins, 25
Matthiessen, Peter, ix
McDonald, Jack, 98
McMurdo Dry Valleys of Antarctica, 4
Medicines, ix
Mesoamerican Barrier Reef, 63
Minot, Francis, 68
Montreal Protocol, xxiii–xxiv
Morefield, James, 17–20
Morgan, Robert, 70
Movile Cave (Romania), 9–10
Mozambique coastline, 57
Muir, John, xiv–xv, xxi, 22, 24, 25–26, 138

National Academy of Sciences, 116
National Audubon Society, 26, 30
National Environmental Policy Act of 1969, 29, 92
National Forest System, 25
National Geographic, 69
National Marine Fisheries Service (NMFS), 53, 72
National Oceanic and Atmospheric Administration (NOAA), 52, 71

National Parks and Conservation Association, 26
National Resources Defense Council, xxii
National Wildlife Federation (NWF), xxii, 26, 30, 105, 113, 130
National Wildlife Refuge System, xii, 25
Natural Resources Defense Council, 29
Natural Science Research Council (Sweden), 113
The Nature Conservancy (TNC), xxii, 56, 57, 98, 125, 126
Naylor, Rosamond, 84
Neo-Malthusians, 27–28
Nets, drift, 75–78
Nets, gill, 75
A New Name for Peace (Shabecoff), 22
New York Times, 22
Nixon, Richard, 28
NMFS (National Marine Fisheries Service), 53, 72
NOAA (National Oceanic and Atmospheric Administration), 52, 71
Noss, Reed, 127
NWF (National Wildlife Federation), xxii, 26, 30, 105, 113

Occupational Safety and Health Act of 1970, 29
Oceans
  overview, 48–49, 65–66
  coastal population of United States, 50–51
  in crisis, 52–53
  fish population decline and, 49–50, 65–66, 80

floor of, 15–16
inexhaustibility fallacy, 84–85
pollution threats to, 50
recommendations, 54
space on Earth's surface, 65
See also Aquaculture; Coral reefs
Ogden, 116–119
Old Faithful, 125
Organizations, environmental, 26
Osborn, Fairfield, 27
Our Nation and the Sea (Stratton), 52
Overfishing, 65–66, 80

Pace, Robert, 123
Pair trawling, 77
Palau (Micronesia), 56–57
Passenger pigeons, ix, xiv
Pauley, Daniel, 79
PCB (polychlorinated-biphenyl), 51
Penicillin, ix
Percent-of-flow water management, 96–97
Peters, Bernardo, 38, 44
Peters, Rodolfo, 44
Peters, Walter, 38
Pew Oceans Commission, 48, 54
Pinchot, Gifford, 22, 24, 25
Pitchfork Ranch (WY), 131–132
Podger, Joe, viii
Pollution of waterways, 29, 108
Pope, Carl, xii
Porpoises, 76–77
Postel, Sandra, 88, 105
Prior appropriation doctrine of water law, 92

Proctor & Gamble, 43
Puget Sound, 51
Purse seining, 71
Pyrolobus fumarii, 5

Qu Geping, 109
Quammen, David, xiv

Rainforest Alliance, 41, 42
Rain forests, tropical, 20
Reagan, Ronald, xxii, 23, 30–31, 48
Recycling, xii
Reefs at Risk (WRI publication), 60
Reefs, coral. *See* Coral reefs
Richards, Daniel, 69
Richter, Brian, 88
Rio Grande Irrigation Co. v. United States, 91
Riparian doctrine of water law, 91–92, 109
River flows, improving, 93
River management
 Benchmarking Methodology, 101
 ecological health and, 90–92
 ethics and, 99–102
 federal options on, 93–95
 percent-of-flow approach to, 96–97
 policies on, 89–90
 states and, 95–99
 U.S. actions and agents for, 94–95
 water use conflicts, 89–90
River of grass (Everglades), 116
Rivers for Life (Postel and Richter), 88
Roberts, Callum, 70
Robinet, Jon, 129

Robinett, Debbie, 129
Rockhopper nets, 78
Rogers Charitable Fund, 43
Rogers Family Coffee Companies, 43
Roosevelt, Theodore, xiii, 22, 23–24, 35, 138

Safina, Carl, 74, 78
Salm, Rod, 55, 56–58
 See also Coral reefs
Sand County Almanac (Leopold), 28
Scheidt, Dan, 122
Schwarzenegger, Arnold, xi
Scott, Robert F., 3
Sea bass, 77–78
Seabrook, John, 67
Shabecoff, Philip, 22
Shade-coffee farms
 overview, 37
 bird-species supported by, 40–41
 certification for, 42–43
 consumer education challenge, 46
 fair-trade for, 44–45
 Finca Irlanda coffee farm, 38–39
 history of coffee growing, 39
Shader, Gina, 129–130
Shrimp farming, 83, 84
Sierra Club, xii, 26
Silent Spring (Carson)
 overview, 138
 arrogance of controlling nature, 144
 Carson's influence, xxi, 23, 28
 changes too rapid for nature, 140
 chemicals in endless stream, 140–141
 contamination of environment, 139, 141

INDEX

DDT, a biocide, 141
failure of poisons, 143
limited awareness of threat, 142
noninvasive chemicals a choice, 143
Skirving, William, 62
SLIMEs (subsurface lithoautotrophic microbial ecosystems), 7–8
Smithsonian Migratory Bird Center, 41, 42
Solar energy, 10
South Florida Water Management District, 122
Southwest Florida Water Management District, 96
Species. *See* also *species by name* (e.g., birds, dolphins).
classification of, 13–15
discovery of new, 17–20
extinction of, ix
number of, 14–15
proliferation of, 10–11
Starbucks, 44
Steinbeck, John, 68
Steneck, Robert, 80
Stockwell, Sally, 148
Stolzenburg, William, 125
Strategic Ignorance (Pope), xii
Stratton Commission, 52
Stripmining the Seas (film) (LaBudde), 76
Strontium 90, 139
subsurface lithoautotrophic microbial ecosystems (SLIMEs), 7–8
Supreme Court, U.S., 99

Sustainable Fisheries Act (1996), 65
Systematists (classification biologists), 12

TCRC (Transforming Coral Reefs Conservation), 56
Thoreau, Henry David, xxi, 22, 24–25, 138
Three Gorges Dam (China), 109–110
TNC. *See* The Nature Conservancy
Tolme, Paul, 37
TransFair, 44
Trawling, pair, 77
Turnell, Jack, 131–132, 133
Turnell, Lilli, 132

Ultrathermophiles, 5–6
Union of Concerned Scientists and Physicians for Social Responsibility, 30
United States v. *Rio Grande Irrigation Co.*, 91
University of Maine, 151
U.S. Army Corps of Engineers, 119–121
U.S. Constitution, 92, 93
USDA (U.S. Department of Agriculture), 23
U.S. Department of Agriculture (USDA), 23
U.S. Division of Forestry, 22
U.S. Environmental Protection Agency (EPA), 23, 28
U.S. Fish and Wildlife Service, 123, 135

U.S. Supreme Court, 99
USCRTF (U.S. Coral Reef Task Force), 56
Usufructory water rights, 92

Vernal pool conservation overview, 145–146
blue-spotted salamander, 150
habitat management guidelines for, 151–152
significance of, 147–149
volunteer program, 148–149, 151–152
Vietnam, 40
VIP (Maine Audubon's Very Important Pool) project, 148
Volunteerism. *See* Vernal pool conservation
Vostok, Lake (Antarctica), 9

Wading bird population, decline of, 121
Washington Department of Ecology v. *Jefferson County*, 99
Washington Sea Grant Program, 74
Water management. *See* River management
Water rights, 92
"Watersheds of the World" (WRI Worldwatch), 111
Watt, James G., 31
Wetland of International Importance (Everglades), 116
Wetlands, small. *See* Vernal pool conservation
Wigington, Robert, 98
Wilderness Society, The, 26

Wildlife Conservation Society, 145
Wille, Chris, 41, 42, 43
Wilson, Edward O.
    on biodiversity, xiv, xxiv
    on conservation policy, xxiii, 2–3
    on ethical codes, 100
    on shade-grown coffee, xii
Wolves, 131, 133–134
World Commission on Dams, 89
World Heritage Site (Everglades), 116
World Resources Institute (WRI), 60, 111

World Summit on Sustainable Development (Johannesburg), 113
World Watch Institute, 37
World Wildlife Fund (WWF), xxii
WRI (World Resources Institute), 60, 111
WWF (World Wildlife Fund), xi, xii–xiii, xix–xx
Wyoming Stockgrowers Association, 131

Yangtze River Basin, 109

Yellowstone National Park, xxi, 6, 25, 123
    overview, 125
    carnivore-livestock conflicts in, 129–130
    ecoregional perspective, 132
    ecosystem in conflict, 130–132
    establishment of, xxi, 25
    plan for, 126–127
    residential development of, 127–129
    story of wolf B58, 126, 135
    wide-ranging carnivores lost, 131
    wolf debate, 133

ABOUT THE CONTRIBUTORS

YAEL CALHOUN is a graduate of Brown University and received her M.A. in Education and her M.S. in Natural Resources Science. Years of work as an environmental planner have provided her with much experience in environmental issues at the local, state, and federal levels. Currently she is writing books, teaching college, and living with her family at the foot of the Rocky Mountains in Utah.

Since 2001, DAVID SEIDEMAN has served as editor-in-chief of *Audubon* magazine, where he has worked as an editor since 1996. He has also covered the environment on staff as a reporter and editor for *Time*, *The New Republic*, and *National Wildlife*. He is the author of a prize-winning book, *Showdown at Opal Creek*, about the spotted owl conflict in the Northwest.